Practical Publicity

PRACTICAL PUBLICITY

How to Boost Any Cause

David Tedone

THE HARVARD COMMON PRESS
Harvard and Boston, Massachusetts

The Harvard Common Press
535 Albany Street
Boston, Massachusetts 02118

Printed in the United States of America

Library of Congress Cataloging in Publication Data
Tedone, David.
   Practical publicity.

   Bibliography: p.
   Includes index.
   1. Publicity.   I. Title.
HM263.T38   1983   659.2   82-23364
ISBN 0-916782-36-0
ISBN 0-916782-35-2 (pbk.)

10   9   8   7   6   5   4   3   2   1

Contents

Preface

GETTING publicity is simple if you have enough money.
You need only to pick up the phone and hire a professional publicist. But few small, nonprofit groups are independently wealthy; in fact, most have learned to survive on terribly meager resources. Publicity, no matter how important, often becomes a low priority for them—occasionally a press release is issued, or a meeting is held. Few groups have long-range publicity strategies, and often their important messages are ill-prepared or inaccurately reported due to lack of money and know-how. As a publicist who has worked with many small, nonprofit groups, I have always felt the need for a simple, straightforward manual on publicity. This book is not for professionals; the techniques it covers are well known to them. Rather, it is addressed to the many part-time, volunteer publicists who are working for worthy causes and relying on limited resources.

In writing this book I have been assisted by many people who deserve mention here. They include Arthur J. Rocque, Jr., and Diane Giampa of the Connecticut Department of Environmental Protection; Lorraine DiSimone of Zero Population Growth; Susan Berger of the Alcohol Prevention Center; Mary Janet Hillary of the Massachusetts Department of Environmental Quality Engineering; Norman Geis; Sarah Belcher of Parental Stress Line; Richard Thornton of the University of Connecticut; Jerome Grossman; Susan Gatchalk of Jewish Big Brother/Big Sister; Mark Selig of Fay Foto; Bill Bird; Deborah Burke of the Massachusetts Adoption Resource Exchange; Karen Rouse of the American Cancer Society; Suzanne Gabriel of Shady Hill School; Janet Ferone of NOW; John P. Callan, M.D.; Attorney Paul N. Shapera; Susan Miron of ABCD, Inc.; Nancy McGraw of Kenyon and Eckhardt; Thomas Gariepy of WFSB-TV; Nancy Novelline of WNEV-TV; Steve Hausman of WCOZ; Bill Porter of WROL; Randy Kirshbaum of WBCN; David MacNeill and Ted Jones of WCRB; WBZ-TV; the *Boston Globe*; the *Boston Herald*; the *Washington Post*; and the *Chicago Sun Times*. Special thanks are due Susan Heinrich, who typed much of my work, and Linda Ziedrich, who edited my rough manuscript.

1.

Publicity and the Practical Publicist

A N OLD story about a deaf boxer named Dummy Mahan and his manager and fight promoter, Fred (Windy) Windsor makes an important point about publicity. In the 1920s Dummy Mahan was slated to fight the champion, Mushy Callahan, for the junior world welterweight title in Los Angeles. The press wasn't showing much interest, ticket sales were soft, and Windy Windsor knew exactly what was needed—a little publicity!

"A little publicity?" Dummy must have asked. "Yeah," signed Windy, "we're gonna drop you from an airplane with a parachute." Dummy shrugged his shoulders. Windy Windsor explained, to Dummy and to the press, that a prominent ear doctor had told him that "free falling through great volumes of space can restore hearing." The press began to nibble. It'll be good for Dummy, Windy boasted; the kid will be able to hear the cheers of the crowd. It'll be great for publicity and ticket sales, he thought; the reporters will surely turn out to cover it.

As it turned out, the stunt was successful—Dummy Mahan got plenty of press coverage after his chute failed to open. Though he was only deaf at the beginning of the stunt (as the punch line goes), Dummy was now dead. Windy Windsor had pulled a publicity coup. If only he still had a fighter to compete in the match.

Perhaps this story, if true, exaggerates the pitfalls of ill-conceived publicity stunts, but it makes a persuasive argument in support of practical publicity. Puffery, flackery, and hype are not what practical publicity is about. In the end, hyped-up publicity does more damage than good, especially if you aim to promote a serious cause. Inflating a serious cause in your media campaign, or distorting its significance with a lot of gimmickry, will often make your cause look foolish and will ultimately destroy the credibility of your organization. A circus under a big top may get your annual rally a lot of attention, but what serious communicator wants to be identified with clowns and bears that ride around on tricycles? Once your credibility is lost, you will quickly find that your publicity and news releases have become radioactive—no editor will touch them.

When most people think about publicity, unfortunately, they remember the stunts, the hype, or the illusion—to use Jimmy Breslin's phrase, the art of "blue smoke and mirrors." What they fail to realize is that publicity—good, solid, practical publicity—makes up a large portion of the "news" that we hear everyday, from the weather blurb in the morning newspaper to major stories on the evening network news. "Soft news," as reports generated by publicity are called, forms the foundation of the information we receive from the major media. Like a supporting actor who is never in the limelight but always performs well, publicity is solidly entrenched in the news industry. Reporters and news directors depend on it. Good publicity is never recognized by the public; it passes as "hard news."

When you take on the role of publicist, your job is to open lines of communication. You became at once an advocate, promoter, and public spokesperson. And although good publicity is not necessarily sedate, pious, or unimaginative, it still must be responsible, valuable, and credible. As you might expect, the more important your cause and goal, the more responsible and credible your publicity must be.

Publicity is the business of attracting public attention to any group, person, product, or cause. Your public, which can be large or small, can be reached through a variety of media and techniques. Publicity can effectively promote or acutely damage a cause or organization, depending on the actual messages communicated, the way they are communicated, and the way the public understands them. Effective publicity has a positive influence on the people it ultimately reaches; it communicates information that they need or are pleased to receive.

The most effective publicity is that which finds a receptive audience, so properly targeting your information is crucial. Publicity gets best results when it has something to offer—some information that people find interesting and appealing. Moreover, the context in which the message is communicated—the media outlet—is often as important as the message itself. A poorly transmitted message is about as effective as no message. Today's audiences are media-wise, and they are not inclined to pay attention to any old blurb. In the arena of mass communication, the ability to reach many individuals is accompanied by an increased potential for message distortion. There is no guarantee that you will get the attention of the public you desire, let alone have the time to get your point across. Publicity can be a game of seconds, and it falls to the practical publicist to strengthen the thrust of the information and target it effectively.

The importance of publicity, especially for nonprofit groups, is magnified by the complexity of our system of mass communication. As individuals in a technological society, we receive hundreds of messages daily from impersonal sources. The mass media have become ingrained in our modern society; they have become each person's link to the rest of society and the world. If you have an important message to relate, you cannot just "take it to the people" by standing on a street corner and appointing yourself town crier. Try it sometime: most people will not even believe you're sane, let alone listen to what you have to say. Unless a message comes through an established medium or a profesional-looking event, it has very little credibility. The world of mass communication has imposed a superstructure around our personal worlds—an elaborate system of talking and listening. Although that system has made it easier to disseminate information to large numbers of people, it has complicated the task of the publicist, who must fully understand the system's intricate methods in order to choose wisely among them.

Audience indifference and competition for audience interest have further complicated the role of the publicist, making it difficult to gain access to the media no matter how important your message. Today's lowly publicist must compete with professional media experts, communicators, advertisers, reporters, press agents, and dozens of others in the business of mass communication, most of whom have much greater resources than the average publicist for a small organization. We are in the midst of a so-called communications revolution, and our country is rapidly being transformed from an industrial society to a communications society. Some estimate that as much as 50 percent of the entire work force is currently employed in the communications industry. The communications revolution is having, and will continue to have, profound effects on our lives. For this reason even the most modest of organizations need good publicists.

With the large cutbacks in governmental funding, many grants and financial advantages once given to public interest groups are no longer available. Because many such groups are in serious financial trouble, they are turning in increasing numbers to private corporations, their own members, and the general public for funds. It only stands to reason that most of the limited private donations will go to the established organizations; since they have been around a while, their identity and purpose are recognized, at least, by the majority of potential donors. Of the few small, young groups that can hope to collect private donations, those that aggressively pursue publicity activities will probably fare the best. Even if a group is to rely solely on funds from its members, it must keep them informed of its activities so that they will continue to offer support.

As many organizations perish from lack of funds, it becomes ever more important to affirm the vitality of your group, lest the public, not hearing about you, think that you too no longer exist. It may be unfair, but the common opinion is that if you haven't survived, then your cause was probably not worth maintaining anyway. The best, most cost-effective way to make people aware of your continued existence is to continue to make headlines. A friend of mine, whose organization has felt the sting of recent economic woes, found this out the hard way. While lobbying at the state capitol she identified her affiliation to a legislator. "I thought you were dead!" he snapped. It's difficult to advance your cause when your group is thought to be extinct.

The key to promoting your cause through practical publicity is building a campaign from the ground up, brick by brick, until you have a solid, well-organized publicity program. Such a program is not created overnight; it is constructed gradually, until the most effective techniques are fully utilized and the most beneficial relationships have been established. Practical publicity is designed to maximize financial and human resources.

A publicity campaign can have any one of a number of objectives. These objectives should be determined before you begin your campaign. What does your group need? Members, financial support, public interest? You may simply want to establish a public identity, or you may have larger aims, such as educating the community on certain social, health, economic, or political issues. Publicity can help develop public awareness of your group's services and motivate people to use them. It can encourage public participation by attracting new members, financial support, and volunteers. It can activate existing club members who have, for one reason or another, become complacent, uninterested, or distracted. Publicity can also be used to counteract negative public perceptions and attitudes, such as racial prejudice, or to enhance a maligned public image. It can focus the public's attention on certain recognized problems or even identify injustices that would otherwise go overlooked. Publicity translates into activity and real clout by affecting the consciousness of many individuals, by creating and expanding an informed constituency.

Publicity and the News

In order to effectively prepare and place publicity notices, you need an understanding of what constitutes news. News value, or newsworthiness, is a crucial factor in determining what gets printed in newspapers and what gets broadcast. Although these terms are applied loosely to a wide variety of events, certain general definitions hold true. In the broadest sense, any information previously unknown and potentially interesting to the public it is intended for can be considered news. Producers and editors exercise a lot of individual discretion in determining what is or is not news. But you can bet that anytime the public interest factor is high, the story will be judged to have news value. Editors gauge audience interest by determining the importance and the relevance of the potential news item. If an event will clearly have widespread effects, as would the outbreak of a war, its importance and, therefore, its newsworthiness is unquestioned. The more people who are affected, the more news value the event has. Editors also consider the relevance of major events as a key to determining newsworthiness. For instance, a war breaks out in the Middle East that has repercussions in the United States. It affects many people directly in the Middle East; it will have indirect consequences, both political and economic, on our country, and the fighting is inherently dramatic and interesting. Its importance would be boosted if one of the warring countries were an ally of the United States, were using U.S. weapons, or were asking for U.S. support. The story immediately becomes "big" because it is important, interesting, and relevant to U.S. audiences.

Now another story breaks. Reggie Jackson is traded from the New York Yankees. The story warrants coverage, but nowhere near the coverage that the war warrants. For one thing, the trade does not directly affect very many people; it does not change our lives. It does have public interest in that Reggie Jackson is publicly known. Baseball itself, a very popular sport, adds to the story's public interest value. The story has human interest, as well—the baseball player's large salary is a juicy tidbit. Although the story would have no great appeal for those uninterested in sports, among sports enthusiasts, or fans of the New York Yankees, the story would have a lot of interest. It would have even more interest for someone who happens to be a member of the Yankees' team. Obviously, the media in New York would treat the story differently from the media in Little Rock, Arkansas—because public interest is apt to be much higher in New York.

Many editors use the "Ward system" for identifying and rating the news value of stories. Walter Ward, a professor of mass communications at Oklahoma State University, devised a system of categorizing events by certain elements. These elements can help you determine which stories generated by your organization have potential news value.

> *Impact news element*, in an event that affects a lot of people or has profound historical significance, such as a Middle Eastern war.

> *Magnitude news element*, in any story that involves large numbers, such as those sometimes evidenced in attendance records, or profit and loss statements. Anything that can be quantified as an extremely large figure has a magnitude news element. A good example is the population of China.

> *Known principals news element*, in news involving any well-known personality, such as Reggie Jackson or a media figure.

Oddity news element, in any event that is strange, bizarre, or unusual, such as the birth of Siamese twins.

Conflict news element, in any story that involves two or more opposing parties, such as a debate or march involving both the proponents and opponents of legal abortion.

If your organization is local, most of your news stories will lack the inherent news value of national events. If you effectively focus on the local media, however, you will find that there is ample community interest in your information to warrant a publicity program. Many of your group's activities will be considered news; announcements of them will be locally broadcast and printed in the local newspapers. Local media and the community at large are usually interested in meetings, rallies, seminars or other educational activities, and open houses. Public statements on local affairs, awards given and received, funding drives, calls for membership, and the appointment and resignation of organization officials also generate considerable interest. Announcements of the availability of speakers whose services are free, films for loan, and the findings of reports and surveys that you may have conducted, as well as petition drives, and participation in and support for national or international causes, certainly have news value in a community. There is really no limit to the activities that can generate publicity, especially if your group is well organized and energetic.

A story may derive its newsworthiness from its entertainment value, educational value, human interest, or historical significance. Thus, although editors and broadcasters use much personal discretion in determining what is news and therefore worthy of coverage, the astute publicist can gauge the news value of his or her announcements by examining the setting and relevance of the story and considering the size of the potential audience. Prepare your announcements and decide where to send them in accordance with these considerations.

Publicity is often confused with advertising, which is

simply publicity that you pay for. By renting column space in a newspaper or magazine or buying air time, you pay for the chance to sell a product or service. The advertising industry is the backbone of the commercial media; it pays most of the cost of printing your newspaper. (All the quarters we pay for our daily paper account for only about one-third of its printing cost.) What the advertisers pay to support the newspapers, of course, consumers repay through increased prices for advertised goods. Nonetheless, magazines, radio, and television stations are kept in business through advertising.

The major drawback to advertising, besides the direct cost, is that it lacks the credibility of a news story. Americans have developed some sophistication toward the media and tend to be skeptical of ads. The public usually trusts news stories, however, whether or not they warrant that trust. As a result, a publicity announcement that sounds like a direct advertisement is less credible and therefore less effective than it could be. And it often does not get free space or time. But when a publicity blurb crosses over that mysterious line into the category of news, it becomes much more persuasive.

Although publicists are trying to sell something—whether a cause, event, or organization—they should restrain from using the hard-sell techniques of advertisers. Instead, they should seek to inform and educate. This subtle difference in approach is often the key to producing effective publicity. When the Red Cross publicizes its blood pressure clinic and asks for a donation, we believe it will provide the service faithfully and use our money properly. Why? Because the Red Cross has established its credibility over many years. Its blurb is much like an advertisement, but editors consider it a public service announcement because the Red Cross is a nonprofit organization. Even if yours is a profit-making group, it can reap substantial benefits by setting up a "public service" promotion campaign, designed to help establish its public identity and credibility through news, not advertising. A reputation thus established is most valuable; it will win your group rewards for years to come.

In short, publicity announcements can take the form of either news stories or advertisements—but effective publicity is news-oriented.

The Publicist's Role

Your external role as publicist may be easier to establish than your internal role. How does the publicist fit into an organization? This often overlooked detail can ultimately determine the effectiveness of a publicity campaign. In order for an organization to benefit from publicity, proper consideration must be given to the publicist. As official spokesperson, you must be aware of every aspect of your organization; you should communicate with participants at all levels—from the president and board to the members and office workers—and you should make yourself accessible. You cannot afford to be caught off guard by the media or the public, and you often must search out information internally before it can be communicated externally. If you are isolated from key decisions, your informational program will suffer. If you do not control the flow of information, then it will probably not be channeled properly. If you are not thoroughly familiar with and directly involved in your group's activities, then you will not be able to effectively represent that group.

As publicist you should always be the first to know—you should act as a clearinghouse for incoming and outgoing information. If possible, you should have direct access to decision makers and unlimited opportunities to advise on the direction, activities, and public image of your organization. You should be consulted and involved in the planning and scheduling of all activities. Publicity has to be a central goal, to which everyone continually contributes; otherwise you will be ineffective. Positive results occur in direct proportion to the amount of effort expended.

You will find described here a complete system for developing and maintaining a practical publicity campaign aimed to take advantage of the special opportunities available to nonprofit organizations. However, the overall method could be adapted for commercial enterprises, with some modification. The principles and techniques are drawn from actual publicity campaigns, and they are discussed in detail to enable do-it-yourselfers to match the results of professionals. This book discusses ways to formulate objectives— and strategies to accomplish these objectives. It also analyzes ways to evaluate, develop, and employ specific tactics, such as speakers bureaus, seminars, films, conferences, media interviews, public service announcements (PSAs), press releases, newsletters, publicity networks, mailing lists, displays, slide shows, media kits, brochures, posters, speeches, editorials, and letters to the editor. These tactics are not simply enumerated and defined; they are evaluated in detail to enable you to choose among them wisely and to get the most from your efforts. After all, the cost of running a publicity campaign effectively is very high, and in these budget-conscious days, nonprofit publicists must keep a wary eye on the bottom line. The focus of this book is on doing these things for less. Cost-cutting measures are described, and a sample budget is provided.

Each chapter examines a different subject and tells you not only what to do, but how to do it. For instance, the complicated task of determining which newspapers and other publications to use is examined, and a handy guide for categorizing publications is presented. The nuts and bolts of practical publicity are also described, specifically in Chapter 4 ("Words and Photos"), which offers many examples of effective press releases and photos. The examples are analyzed for content and technique to illustrate why some materials work and others do not.

Because of the expansion of radio and television and the special opportunities for nonprofit groups with these publicity outlets, two chapters have been devoted to the electronic media. They describe how to zero in on the stations, what programs to use, and how to contact them. Methods for gaining air time are also discussed, and examples of PSAs and citizen editorials are provided, along with detailed explanations of how to write, develop, and deliver them. Tips on interviewing, such as what to wear and how to prepare your remarks, are specifically geared to dealing with the electronic media.

Every serious publicity campaign must have its own publications, and although printing is often the most costly aspect of a campaign, there are ways to help keep those costs to a minimum without sacrificing the overall quality of the publications. Suggestions on design, layout, and dealing with the printer are made, and point-by-point instructions for putting out a newsletter—perhaps your most important publication—are included.

Of course, an effective campaign makes good use of person-to-person communication techniques, such as display booths, speakers bureaus, canvassing, seminars, and open forums. Effective ways to meet the public, establish contacts, and handle yourself in public are included. These personal interactions, although time-consuming, are often the most rewarding. Because you are most vulnerable in these situations, you must make it a point to communicate effectively and to make a good impression. Conducting a publicity campaign by meeting the people, face to face, will often build the strongest constituency and establish enduring support.

Networking, or the art of building interest and support through grass-roots participation, is described in detail in a separate chapter. Various methods, using phone trees, mailing lists, volunteers, petitions, membership involvement, and coalitions, are discussed. Although they may be difficult to establish, networks can bring an avalanche of support.

The book concludes with an annotated list of important information sources, standard publicity tools of which the practical publicist should be aware.

Needless to say, you will not find a chapter on gimmicks and stunts in this book. P.T. Barnum may have been a master publicist in his day, but his techniques of hokum and razzmatazz would probably be considered a joke today. Don't get me wrong—publicity doesn't have to be grim. There is always room for lightheartedness and fun—if you are promoting something lighthearted and fun, such as a circus. The importance of decorum cannot be overstressed.

If my advice doesn't dissuade you from publicity tricks, gimmicks, and stunts, then you might consider the following story. A few years ago, a community theater group decided to put on the play *An Attempt at Flying*. Well, someone had "a great idea" to publicize the event. The group rented a giant hot-air balloon, emblazoned the play's title across it, and persuaded the director to go for a brief ride. The cast and crew were to hold the ropes, let the balloon ascend one hundred feet or so, and get a great photo. The day they chose turned out to be somewhat windy, and they at first had trouble trying to get the heater, which produces the hot air, to function properly. (In the theater they call this foreshadowing.) But eventually they got it to work, the balloon filled with air, and the pilot and director climbed aboard.

As the ropes were being let out, a stiff breeze caught the balloon. The crew was lifted off the ground and had to release the ropes. The balloon rose so quickly and so high that it was soon nearly out of sight. The "attempt at flying" violated Federal Aviation Administration flight regulations and posed a hazard to airplanes, and the pilot and director were nearly frostbitten and asphyxiated in the thin air. Eventually able to control the balloon by releasing the hot air, they descended, though nowhere near the launch point. In fact, they landed in a schoolyard filled with children. School officials were enraged that they endangered the children, the police slapped them with a summons, and the FAA fined them.

The theater group never got a photo, but it did get some press coverage—not the kind it expected. The newspapers were not exactly admiring; rather, they dwelled on the danger and overall poor planning of the stunt. But, then, someone had had this "great idea" for getting publicity, and who could resist giving it a try? After all, it was only an attempt at flying.

2.

Strategy and Tactics

STARTING up a spanking new publicity program can be bewildering, especially if you have little experience to fall back on. Faced with meager human and financial resources, and often pressed for immediate results, most would-be publicists try to cope by generating a flood of haphazard information. Sparks begin to fly, newsletters and press releases are cranked out, petitions begin circulating, a bevy of canvassers start combing the neighborhood, posters appear, and you suddenly feel as if you are in the center of a tornado you cannot control. Even though a lot of activity is taking place, you question how much is actually translating into publicity, and whether the effect of your publicity is positive or negative. The scenario is a familiar one to many publicists; you're in the so-called fifth dimension of the publicity world, a kind of communications twilight zone where anything can happen.

The goal of the practical publicist is to avoid entering that never-never land—by implementing a prudent campaign, by controlling the flow of information, and by keeping expenses to a minimum. To accomplish that goal you must maximize the use of time and labor—and money. It becomes important not only to prepare your reports and target your activities properly, but also to coordinate your efforts for maximum results. You must establish a basic strategy with realistic schedules and objectives. You should adopt tactics that work well together and relate to the whole campaign. Without proper planning, most of your activities will end up being ineffective or damaging. Lack of planning can be deadly to a publicity program.

Many publicists do not understand the difference between tactics and strategy, or what I consider the heart and soul of practical publicity. These are important concepts to consider when planning a publicity campaign. *Strategy* refers to the overall direction and scope of your program, your plan of operation; it defines schedules, target groups, and ultimate goals. *Tactics* refers to the nuts and bolts of the campaign, techniques such as developing newspaper and television contacts, publishing a newsletter, establishing a speakers bureau, and initiating a petition drive. The strategy sets the tone and course; the tactics are the vehicles for carrying out the strategy.

Determining Your Goals

Developing a strategy should always begin with a bit of introspection—a serious and objective look at what you, or your group, has to offer to the public. Why does the public need to concern itself about your cause? Why should people care? Just because you feel strongly about certain issues does not mean that a significant portion of the community feels the same way, or that these issues are worth considering. Before starting up the campaign, you should ask yourself, "Am I being self-serving, or do I really have something valuable to offer?" You should be able to come up with a list of public concerns that you can address and benefits that you can provide.

For instance, if you belong to a newly formed group opposed to the construction of a hazardous waste treatment plant in your community, you should be able to identify several major issues for public consideration; for example:

Your community has already allowed the construction of several major industrial complexes.

Those complexes have placed a strain on certain neighborhoods and reduced the quality of life there.

The new facility will affect many people in the community.

Your community produces no hazardous wastes; thus, the choice of siting seems illogical.

The potential health impacts of the new facility have not been explored, though many children live in the community.

The fact that your community is made up of lower-middle-class residents may have something to do with the choice of siting. In a neighboring community that is more affluent, the project was turned down.

The plant would provide certain tax benefits.

New jobs have been promised.

You question the credibility of your town's permitting agency, which has a history of poorly planned projects.

Obviously, all of these issues are serious and easily warrant the attention of your group and its publicity campaign. Your major concern is that the project will affect many people. Prior public awareness regarding a project of such magnitude is crucial; once the facility has been constructed, there will be little recourse if something unforeseen occurs. Whether the people care or not, therefore, they should be kept abreast of the developments, or perhaps "educated" about potential consequences. If your group can adequately address the issues listed here, then you will no doubt have plenty of work to do and ample justification for your efforts. In fact, you will probably be hard pressed to come up with activities that can adequately communicate the range and complexity of the issues.

You must also evaluate your group's ability to address certain issues, such as the health impacts. If you do not have expertise on health issues, you are probably better off not generating publicity about them. You may quote the statements of others concerning the health impacts, but if you attempt to promote unscientific opinions you will only end up distorting the issue and discrediting your organization. You would be completely justified in raising the health question, however, so long as you refrain from fomenting hysteria. You should look externally and internally at your role as public communicator.

Let us consider another example. You are responsible for promoting a nonprofit bicycle club, whose major functions are to organize weekend bicycling trips and to generate interest in bicycling as a form of recreation. What messages should your publicity campaign generate? In the first place, your activities do not affect many people; you are promoting a recreational activity for the enjoyment and benefit of participants only. You can perhaps claim to promote exercise and good health, but that is about the extent of the public benefits you provide.

The publicity campaign has one primary objective: to generate participants. The objective is not as complex or socially significant as that of the hazardous waste facility. As a result, the club does not need a broad range of publicity activities. Its objective could probably be accomplished through a program of community calendar listings, bulletin board advertisements, affiliation with a local high school or organization such as the Young Men's Christian Association, press releases announcing upcoming trips, and direct mailings to members or past participants. You would not want to launch a full-scale rally with political speakers. And although you might circulate a handbill listing the many benefits of adopting bicycling as the community's primary mode of transportation, your club would not want to begin a campaign calling for the ban of automobiles. Such a campaign would be a little beyond the scope of your organization, and in essence a little absurd. In short, your publicity activities should accurately reflect the scope of your organization—no more, no less.

Identifying Your Audience

Deciding whom you want to reach is another crucial step in developing your publicity plans. More than any other aspect of the campaign, your audience helps define the type of program you should run and the direction it should take. Trying to reach the "general public" is not good enough: you must put a face on your intended audience. This will help you focus on appropriate media and present your information effectively.

Whom you should target for your publicity efforts depends largely on your goal. The audience appropriate for the bicycle club's publicity program can be narrowed down relatively simply. People who might be interested are in relatively good physical condition and able to engage in bicycling. This means they are young, for the most part, say between the ages of sixteen and forty-five. You should aim your messages mainly at adults, because your weekend-long trips would otherwise require parental approval and a chaperone; however, you may want to welcome children who are accompanied by an adult. Your primary public, therefore, is composed of relatively young and physically able adults. You may try to reach children in the hope that they will in turn influence their parents, but the results of such an approach would be less favorable.

Of your adult group, you will get the most interest and participation from people who can afford the equipment (a bicycle, sleeping bag, and so on) and the leisure time. This limits you primarily to people who have few household responsibilities (such as several children to care for) and fairly secure finances. The major exceptions to that profile will be young adults (between the ages of eighteen and twenty-two, perhaps), including college students, who are often strapped financially but who use bicycles. Most students are not tied down with responsibilities, and many enjoy bicycling as a sport. You can also zero in on people who enjoy outdoor activities such as hiking and camping. You can then devise a list of target groups in order of importance. Your list should look something like the following:

Young, professional adults with athletic and outdoor interests

College students

Children

Reaching your key group—young adults with athletic and outdoor interests—is your first priority. You should seek publicity outlets that are sure to reach them, such as a local alternative newspaper that caters to a young audience, radio stations featuring top-forty or rock music, some in-house business publications, athletic clubs and gyms, stores that carry sporting goods, and bicycle shops. You can reach college students through student newspapers and radio stations, direct mailings, and flyers or posters on campus. Children should not be a high priority, although they do influence their parents. But they can be reached best on playgrounds, by local TV, through publications written for children, and through their schools. You will want to direct some announcements at the general public, of course, to reach those potentially interested persons who are not reached by the aforementioned outlets, and those athletic organizations and bicycle shops of which you are unaware. You can then develop different approaches for specific groups and for the general public.

The same process of identifying target groups can be applied to other organizations, such as one concerned with promoting birth control. Here you can readily identify direct and indirect target groups and subgroups.

Women of childbearing age, and men (direct)

Married couples (subgroup)

Teenaged girls and, secondarily, boys (subgroup)

College students, primarily women but also men (subgroup)

Physicians (indirect)

Counselors and social workers (indirect)

Obviously, women of childbearing age represent the most directly affected and potentially interested segment of the public. Men are also involved in birth control measures, but they are only secondary targets because women, it is commonly recognized, are more responsible than men when it comes to birth control. (Unfair as it may be, women's greater burden of responsibility in birth control is a practical reality in our society.)

To accomplish your goal of promoting birth control, reaching women is crucial. Besides releasing information to the general public through such outlets as your local daily, and besides reaching all recognized women's organizations, you can go further by identifying subgroups. Married couples can be identified by obtaining the town's record for marriage licenses. Teenaged girls, as well as boys, are a problematic group, but they can be reached through radio stations, TV, high schools, and publications aimed at high school students. They can also be reached through youth clubs in the neighborhood and through their parents. College students are a relatively easy group to reach because of the many media outlets available in college communities.

You should single out physicians as an indirect target and provide them with information regarding the social issues of birth control. Although physicians probably have plenty of information on the types of contraceptives available, they should be aware of your group so they can refer patients to you. Physicians can be reached through professional journals, by direct mail, and through other outlets such as hospitals and clinics. Other medical workers, like nurses, also represent important groups to target, as do social workers and counselors, whose jobs involve dealing with many people and diverse problems. Such groups can usually be reached through governmental agencies and public and private organizations, including professional associations. Groups that you identify as indirect targets should be made aware of your organization and what it represents, so that when someone needs your help your name will come up.

By putting a face on your audience, you can streamline your efforts: you can tailor your messages, choose your outlets effectively, focus your campaign, and reduce your costs.

The one group that should always be a target of your publicity, no matter what groups are considered priorities, consists of the individuals within your own organization. Too often, the persons who work under the publicist's own roof are overlooked. Not only do they represent a public that should be aware of all the activities and viewpoints of their organization, they also make up a publicity team ready to spread the word to family, friends, acquaintances, and other organizations.

Planning a Schedule

Having set your goals, you should establish the longevity of your project—one year, one month, ongoing—and key dates that will determine the timeliness of your campaign. Dates are important considerations in planning a publicity strategy. If you are working for a project with a specific goal, such as passing legislation or rejecting a construction project, you will find a predetermined schedule that should be applied to your activities. You can link your project thematically to an event in the public's memory—for example, by opening a resource-recovery plant on Earth Day or holding an antinuclear rally on the anniversary of the bombing of Hiroshima.

For instance, I was once involved in a national campaign known as "Year of the Coast." It corresponded with the tenth anniversary of the National Oceanic and Atmospheric Administration (NOAA), and culminated when Congress was considering reauthorizing legislation concerning coastal land use and development. Because one of our prime concerns was the reauthorization, our publicity program had a built-in time frame. The campaign was well orchestrated; hundreds of publicity events occurred nationwide. Both public interest and promotional activities peaked on the day Congress opened debate on the measure, which was passed overwhelmingly. Credit careful planning and scheduling.

The three-phase strategy. If your program is to run for a long time, you may want to consider using a three-phase publicity strategy: a kickoff phase in which you establish a public identity; an expansion or issue-orientation phase; and a culmination phase. In the first phase you'll concentrate on explaining who your group is, where it is situated, how it originated, and what it intends to do. This is your public debut, your introduction to the media and the masses. Politicians frequently refer to the beginning of their campaigns as the "name-recognition" phase. The aim is simply to get the public to recognize their names, which they emblazon on billboards, lawn signs, and placards held on street corners during rush hour, and on which they make all types of witty and not-so-witty puns. The kickoff of any publicity campaign should be aimed at name recognition, a clear goal within reach of most publicists, no matter how meager their resources and experience.

The tactics you should use during this phase are simple and direct, such as issuing press releases, public announcements, flyers, or PSAs, or even holding a kickoff rally (if you can scare up enough of an audience). Events with symbolic significance are particularly effective, such as the promotion of a solar energy campaign on the anniversary of the accident at Three-Mile Island. It is too early, however, to organize a debate on key issues or issue a formal call for public support. You can focus on issues and expansion later, once you have established a public identity.

The expansion phase begins when the general public knows what your group stands for and views it as a credible source of information. You now try to permeate the public consciousness, utilize the media contacts established in the first phase, and expand on the gains you have already made. Your goal is to orient the public toward issues related to your cause. Your tactics become more complicated; you must gain enough public attention and media coverage to explain the issues in detail and make sure your audience understands them. Public debates, seminars, editorials on radio and television, newsletters, and continued use of press releases and PSAs can all be effective. The key is to emphasize issues, to educate and inform. To maintain your credibility, of course, you must make sure that your information is accurate. And to make the most progress, you should meet people face to face.

When you have created an identity, informed a population, and isolated important issues, you will be in a position to wield substantial power. The culmination phase begins. By utilizing your established lines of communication, you can put out a call to your informed constituency, who will help focus the public's attention on your cause. If you are trying to affect passage of legislation, for example, your supporters can be directed to apply pressure on the legislature. The effect is an amplification of your group's pleas—a far greater noise than your group could ever make alone. In this third phase, the culmination, you can use phone trees, newsletters, direct mailings, letters to the editor, letters to politicians, press releases, PSAs, citizen editorials, and media coverage (once your publicity efforts have made your group newsworthy).

Needless to say, all publicity campaigns do not have to conform to the three-phase strategy. You may plan an ongoing program with no end in sight, or a program too short to develop distinct phases. You may not even have specific issues to address or a specific event to influence. Or, perhaps, your program may warrant a much more complex strategy with many phases, two or more of which will be carried out simultaneously. The basic three-phase strategy can serve as an effective framework on which you can build your campaign, or it can be used as a bench mark for evaluating the organization and goals of your program. In either case, it can help organize the publicity process, which has a tendency to go haywire if improperly attended.

Choosing Tactics

The practical publicist can choose among many tactics. Here is a partial list of tactics that can be inexpensively applied:

Citizen editorials—TV, radio, press

Bumper stickers

Phone trees

Seminars

Press releases

Brochures

News stories

Hot lines

News conferences

Speakers bureau

Film library

Slide shows

Newsletters

Displays

Pamphlets

Panel discussions—TV, radio, public

Posters

Impromptu interviews—TV, radio, press

Handouts

Flyers

Talk shows—TV, radio

Public service announcements (PSAs)

Community calendars—TV, radio, press

Direct mail

Media kits

Media contacts

Coalitions

Volunteers

Letters to the editor

Petition drives

Canvassing

All these tactics can be effective when used appropriately; the problem is choosing the ones best suited to the circumstances and implementing them correctly. Select those that best suit your group's goals, abilities, schedule, and budget. As practical publicist, you must always concern yourself with coordination. For example, you would not want to conduct two direct mailings a few days or even a week apart because mailing is expensive. Instead, you would combine the materials in a single mailing. Before holding a seminar or rally, likewise, you would send out press releases and community calendar announcements, and you would include several blurbs in your newsletter. Different tactics often go hand in hand.

Let us return to the three-phase strategy briefly. Tactics that can be used in the first phase to establish public identity may include media kits for developing contacts; news conferences to kick off the campaign; PSAs and press releases; posters, flyers, and community calendars; canvassing or a direct mail campaign; and the first issue of a newsletter.

In the second phase, that of issue orientation, you should choose tactics that will create forums for discussion, and that are necessarily time-consuming. These may include citizen editorials, letters to the editor, a speakers bureau, seminars, and guest appearances on TV and radio programs. To maintain your visibility, you will probably continue to send newsletters, press releases, and PSAs.

In the culminating phase you should make use of your group's notoriety. While maintaining your visibility through PSAs, newsletters, a speakers bureau, guest media appearances, and interviews, you should also seek to amplify your voice by forming coalitions, draw in interested individuals by establishing phone trees, and document your support by conducting petition drives and letter-writing campaigns. You should hold several major news conferences and media events.

A certain amount of flexibility must be maintained no matter which techniques you choose. You cannot ignore the brush fires that, despite your careful planning, may pose serious consequences for your program, nor can you continue using tactics that are not working. Your strategy is not cast in bronze; you should remain sensitive to the often changing demands of your publicity campaign and alter your tactics as the need arises.

Budgeting Time and Money

Allocating time and money is a skill best learned by experience and practice, but you can steer clear of major pitfalls by following a simple method. When budgeting time, your primary consideration should be whether you will be able to perform all the necessary tasks—even the smallest ones—in the time allotted. For example, you want to issue a press release. How much time will it take? If you itemize the tasks involved, you find it entails much more than writing and typing. You will need to reproduce the release, purchase envelopes, produce labels, assemble the mailing (apply the labels and seal the envelopes), and deliver the envelopes to the post office. The amount of time required for these tasks depends on the size of your mailing list—and whether you even have one yet. If your mailing list has been around awhile, you will need to review it ahead of time to ensure that the most appropriate contacts will be receiving the release—and in time to meet their deadlines. If members of your group should review your work, you must allow time for them to read the release and suggest changes. You will have to see to other details, such as filing a copy of the release (or perhaps starting a file), making a copy available to the person who will answer inquiries (if other than yourself), and distributing the release internally. The seemingly simple task of issuing a press release suddenly becomes much more complicated than you expected.

Budgeting time to produce a newsletter is even more complicated. (Obviously, the more complicated the task, the more complicated the schedule.) Aside from researching and writing the copy, preparing graphics, and deciding on a format, you will have to endure internal reviews and possible rewrites. You must allocate enough time for production—typing, typesetting, proofreading, layout, design, and acquiring materials. And agreements with the printer and mailer (if you have one) must be worked out. This involves giving necessary instructions and reviewing proofs before delivery.

After delivery you must also consider accounting time:

who will review the charges and pay the printer? There will be other tasks to do, such as storage and inventory of publications. Assuming that your mailing list has already been made, you will have to update it and reproduce labels. Time must be allocated for applying the labels to newsletters, for sorting and packing, and for securing mailing permits. Once again, postal delivery time should be considered, as well as the time required for filling out forms and paying postage—small details that accumulate. If your messages will become quickly outdated, you should allow several days for delivery in your production schedule. The post office will no doubt return some of the newsletters, which you should use in updating your mailing list. If your messages concern controversial issues, or if you are advertising services or products, you should be prepared to receive correspondence and phone calls.

Every detail, no matter how small, should be considered when you formulate a time schedule. You will understand why when you are coordinating a dozen or so publicity activities occurring simultaneously, and you find yourself with less and less time to spare. The best way to budget your time is to think through the entire procedure and itemize the tasks to be accomplished. Then allocate as realistically as possible the time it will take for each, in units no smaller than fifteen minutes.

Suppose you are preparing a ten-second PSA for television. The amount of time it takes to accomplish the tasks involved may vary considerably, depending on the skill of the person or persons performing them, the organization, the subject matter, and the response from public service directors. Your superiors may only "rubber stamp" your idea, or they may take time to contemplate or discuss it. They may want you to change the thrust of your PSA once it is written, which will of course require extra time. If you already have a well–thought-out and up-to-date list of contacts, reviewing it will require minimal time. Packaging your PSA can be a simple task if you have established formats to follow (letterhead, sample letters of transmittal, and so on) and if background information on your program, as in a fact sheet or newsletter, is already prepared. No matter what, following up with a phone call to every contact will require substantial amounts of time and energy—you can count on having to leave messages, get wrong numbers, wait for return calls, and get put on hold from time to time. It is wise to allow a little extra time for unforeseen delays—due to the photographer's misplacing your illustrations, for example.

Budgeting time thus involves systematically breaking down a project into necessary tasks and allocating time for each. This may sound complicated and time-consuming, but once you go through the process a few times you will find that you can quickly estimate the amount of time required for almost any given task. Occasionally you will have to guess—for example, when you are setting up a new speakers bureau or hot line and cannot predict the public's response. After a month or so, however, you will be able to identify a pattern you can use in adjusting your long-term schedule.

Once your tasks have been itemized and your time allocated, it is relatively simple to determine approximate costs. In figuring costs we exclude labor, assuming that workers are either salaried or volunteer; we are here concerned only with *direct outside* costs, as for postage and materials. If I were to send a ten-second PSA to fifteen television contacts, I might list the following tasks and the corresponding direct outside costs.

Formulate subject matter	No cost
Identify audience	No cost
Discuss with superiors	No cost
Identify appropriate TV outlets	No cost
Phone contacts	If long-distance, costs could reach $15
Write copy	Minimal cost of office supplies, covered by program's general budget
Review copy and rewrite	No cost

Prepare illustration (slide)	Cost of roll of film, art work, developing: $10 to $30
Have copies of slide made	$1.50 per slide, glass-mounted; total, $22.50
Have copy typed and reproduced	No cost
Prepare letter of transmittal	No cost
Prepare envelopes and labels	$ .15 per envelope; total, $2.25. Marginal cost for labels
Include background information	No cost if already prepared; cost of newsletter covered by newsletter budget
Package and label PSA	No cost
Send or deliver to contacts	$ .35 postage per envelope; total, $5.25
Follow up with phone calls	Approximately $15.00
File copy	No cost
Monitor media outlets	No cost

Issuing the PSA would cost $70 to $90, excluding tax and the cost of supplies that would be covered by other budgets—the newsletter budget or the general office supplies budget, for example. Preparing a ten-second PSA is a relatively inexpensive publicity task; when formulating a budget for a more complex project like a newsletter, seminar, or canvass, you will find that itemizing is more difficult and less exact. Sometimes it is wise to increase your estimate by 10 or 20 percent to ensure adequate funds. This general method will help you gauge the overall cost of operating a publicity campaign and figure out what tactics you can afford.

Evaluating Your Progress

The moment of truth for the practical publicist comes when you are asked the ultimate question: "Well, is the publicity program working?" Your strategies and tactics suddenly seem unimportant; in the end, the publicist is judged by results.

The most direct way to evaluate your program is to ask yourself whether your goal has been accomplished. Has your membership increased, has the legislation been passed, have you gotten the needed funding? If your goal has been accomplished, then the answer to the question is simple: "Yes!" But if you have been successful you won't need to tell people so—everyone will assume that the publicity program has worked. And if the program has failed, the question has come too late. It is important to ask the ultimate question yourself—and answer it, too—long before your superiors start wondering about your effectiveness.

There are a few techniques for evaluating your publicity program while it is in progress. These include monitoring the media and documenting the amount and type of coverage (pro or con) ; determining whether your mailing lists or membership rolls have grown; determining whether more people are utilizing your services; conducting general telephone, postcard, or street surveys to gauge public recognition of your group and perception of relevant issues before, during, and after your campaign; measuring the support at rallies and meetings; surveying persons on your mailing list; and noting the number of volunteers you can get involved in letter-writing efforts, petition drives, and so on.

You must read the signs with care; the formation of an opposing group or a statement by the governor in support of your cause may not be a direct result of your publicity. There is no really scientific method that you can rely on in evaluating your program; even the so-called scientific poll is subject to error. It is important to keep in mind that these methods can give you only a general idea of your progress.

3.

Meeting the Press

IT IS difficult to overestimate the importance of the press to the practical publicist. In a newspaper, generally speaking, you will have better chances of landing a news item and having it reach the largest public (for the least cost) than in any other established medium. Nearly every community in the nation has its own newspaper, whether daily, weekly, monthly, or quarterly. And most states have at least one major newspaper that covers events state-wide. Moreover, most newspapers, especially the smaller ones, rely on nonpartisan sources—namely, individuals who pass on bits of information that provide leads for reporters or who furnish stories and press releases that are printed as is. To take advantage of the free coverage offered by newspapers, the practical publicist needs a firm understanding of how the press operates, how to prepare press releases, how to cultivate good relations with the press, and what editors expect from publicists.

Surveying the Local Press

Start by considering the press in your region. The press comprises several media—daily and weekly (and biweekly and triweekly) newspapers, specialty publications, magazines, and wire services—which coexist in most areas. As you begin your publicity campaign, identify the types of press available in your area by consulting the yellow pages of your phone book or one of the directories listed in the last chapter. Go to a newsstand or library and scan the publications that interest you to get an idea of the audiences they address.

Dailies. Daily newspapers aim to cover all topics with news value for the general public. They must search out enough feature stories to fill a new edition every day. Most cities have at least one major daily; some well-known examples are the *Los Angeles Times*, the *Washington Post*, the *Chicago Tribune*, the *New York Times*, the *Detroit Free Press*, the *Philadelphia Inquirer*, and the *Des Moines Register*. Because these newspapers have wide circulations, they offer maximum public exposure—but competition for their column space is intense. Dailies may be published in morning or evening editions, or they may be updated at regular intervals through the day.

Weeklies (and biweeklies, triweeklies, and monthlies). With an emphasis on general news, these too are characterized by their frequency of publication, which is limited because circulations are small. Either the reporters are unable to gather enough interesting news stories to print daily, or the publisher is unable to afford a new issue each day. Weeklies are usually directed at a local community, and they often fill a gap in news coverage left by a large daily, which can devote only a small amount of column space to each of the many communities it serves. The typical weekly is an excellent source of publicity for local groups. Because these newspapers usually have modest staffs and budgets, they are happy to use press releases issued by local groups and provide them with news coverage. There are eight thousand weeklies in the country, according to the American Newspaper Publishers Association. Every major city has several. For example, in Sacramento, California, a capital city with three hundred thousand inhabitants, you find the *Carmichael Citizen*, the *Citrus Heights Bulletin*, the *North Highlander*, the *Sacramento Suburban*, the *San Juan Record*, the *Spacemaker*, and others. These newspapers all fall under the category of the weekly, biweekly, triweekly, or monthly; each covers a special neighborhood, ethnic group, or topic.

Specialty publications. This category includes trade, professional, and technical newspapers and newsletters, alternative publications, college and farm publications, and all other publications aimed at small, well-defined groups with common affiliations or interests. Their topics are various: governmental affairs, construction, chiropractic, ecology, ceramics, business and finance, aviation, and cordage and twine are a few examples. They may be published in a newspaper, newsletter, or even glossy format. Specialty publications are excellent channels for publicity if you are targeting groups with specific interests. For instance, if you wished to publicize a cause or event of particular interest to black Americans, then you would definitely want to have the *National Scene* on your media list; if you were running a wildlife conservation campaign, you would want to have the *Louisiana Conservationist* on your list. Examples of other specialty publications are *Frozen Food Age*, *Robotics Today*, *Shoe Service*, and *Animal Rights Law Reporter*—each catering to a very specific audience. Specialty publications offer both advantages and disadvantages to the practical publicist. If the subject you are publicizing relates to the publication, you can bet that the editors will give you coverage, and that you will thereby reach an interested and highly responsive audience. But often that audience will be very small. It may be clustered in one small locale, or it may be scattered across the country. It is difficult to tailor publicity announcements for such an audience.

General-circulation magazines. These publications are characterized by their formats, usually 8½ by 11 inches in two or more colors on glossy paper. Although there are several general-interest magazines, such as *Time* and *Newsweek,* most magazines cover specific subjects and cater to certain segments of the general readership—though these segments are usually larger and less well-defined than those served by specialty publications. Many of the lesser known magazines, like specialty publications, are related to specific associations, such as the American Chess Federation's *Chess Life and Review. Stereo Review, Runner's World, Working Mother,* and *Forum* are typical of general interest magazines in that their audiences are specific, though large, and scattered across the country. Magazines tend not to be as news-oriented as dailies and weeklies. Instead, they emphasize features; they often print six to eight long stories in a single issue. Their production process is correspondingly lengthy, as it must be to ensure high quality in the finished product, and usually expensive as well. Because they usually need several months lead time before printing an article or photo, magazines are not the best outlets for "late-breaking" news or announcements intended for immediate release.

Wire services. The major wire services are privately owned organizations that function like any large newspaper, with reporters, editors, bureau chiefs, and photographers. There's one difference, though: they never publish any newspapers. Instead, they offer their reporting services to existing publications and television and radio stations worldwide. The major wire services are the Associated Press (AP), United Press International (UPI), and Knight-Ridder. Other wire services, such as the *Los Angeles Times,* the *Chicago Tribune,* and the *Washington Post,* also offer stories throughout the world. AP has several thousand subscribers, and UPI several thousand more; together they boast a potential audience in the hundreds of millions. When UPI prepares a story of national interest (such as a policy statement by the U.S. secretary of state), it is typed on a computer terminal, which then transmits the story (photo as well as copy) to receiver terminals in each of the subscribers' offices. The subscribing newspapers and radio stations then have the option of using the story immediately, holding it for possible future use, or discarding it. Transmittal can be restricted by state or region. A story about an event in New England, for example, may go over only the New England wire, to those subscribers in the six northeastern states. Other stories may be sent only to states on the East Coast, West Coast or Great Lakes, again depending on potential interest. Because wire services have offices all across the country and around the world, their reporters are seemingly ubiquitous; they cover every major event and many minor ones. The wire services complement local reporting by providing firsthand accounts to the *Wyoming Sun*, for example, from as far away as Newport News, Virginia.

Wire services concentrate on big stories, however, especially those concerning national politics, and will not pick up local items unless they have a broad appeal. For the publicist, therefore, wire services serve a function opposite from that of weeklies and other local newspapers. A drawback to using wire services for publicity is that, despite the number of affiliated newspapers, there are no guarantees that any will print your story. The wire service reporter has little or no control once the story is released, so reaching the desired audiences may be difficult.

When addressing a press release, press kit, or conference invitation to newspapers, you should consider the size and character of each paper's audience, the frequency of its publication, and the kind of news it emphasizes. This will help you to determine who will be receiving your information, when they might want to publish it, and, if they do, who will be reading it.

For example, in Boston, a fairly large city with a complex of newspapers serving distinct neighborhoods, there are two major dailies: the *Boston Globe* and the *Boston Herald*. Another daily, the *Christian Science Monitor,* is also located in Boston, but it is written for a national audience. The *Globe* is published every morning and updated in several editions throughout the day. It has a paid circulation of five hundred thousand, and is probably read each day by seven hundred thousand people. It is a comprehensive metropolitan newspaper; it covers events of national and international importance as well as local affairs, and it includes special features such as "Living" and "At Home." As a result, it reaches a large cross section of the population. People from nearly all walks of life and nearly every community in the metropolitan area read the *Globe*.

The only real competition that the *Globe* has in Boston comes from the *Boston Herald*, which is also published every morning. It has a paid circulation of two hundred thousand and is probably read by three hundred thousand people daily. The *Herald* is immediately distinguishable from the *Globe* by its smaller format, many pictures, and condensed news stories; it is known as a tabloid. Although the *Herald,* like the *Globe,* has a general readership, it has a slightly different appeal and focus. The *Herald* is less formal than the *Globe,* with briefer articles and a more personal tone. But either newspaper will effectively publicize an event or cause of general interest. These two papers are considered publicity staples in Boston.

The *Globe* and the *Herald,* of course, cannot cover every neighborhood event in the city of Boston, so several small weeklies exist to fill the gap. They include the *Dorchester Argus Citizen,* the *Dorchester Record,* the *East Boston Times, Jamaica Plain Citizen,* the *South Boston Marshall,* and the *South End News.* If you were trying to get people in certain neighborhoods interested in an event, you would not overlook these small but well-located newspapers. The same holds true for the weeklies that are published in the surrounding towns that make up the metropolitan Boston area. They include:

Allston-Brighton Citizen Item

Arlington Advocate

Belmont Citizen

Belmont Herald

Brookline Chronicle Citizen

Cambridge Express

Cambridge Chronicle

Charlestown Patriot

Chelsea Weekly News

Newton Villager and Transcript

Quincy Sun

Somerville Journal

News-Tribune (in Waltham and Newton)

Watertown Herald

Watertown Sun

Wellesley Townsman

You can see that some of the towns even have competing weeklies. If your news involved a Boston neighborhood or suburb, you could bet that the appropriate weekly would pick it up. Some people might even read your announcement twice, since many of the readers of the weeklies subscribe to the *Globe* or the *Herald*.

Upon identifying all these potential publicity outlets, you would find yet another category of newspaper in the Boston area. This category, which serves ethnic and other special markets, includes:

Armenian Spectator

Banker and Tradesman

Boston Irish News

Boston Ledger (a weekly with a large circulation throughout the metropolitan Boston area)

Boston Phoenix (an alternative weekly that caters to a young audience and focuses on the arts)

Boston Sports Eagle

El Mundo (a Spanish-language newspaper circulated throughout New England)

Gay Community News

German Courier

Greek Sunday News

Hellenic Chronicle (also a Greek-language newspaper)

Irish Citizen

Irish Echo

Italian Item

Jewish Reporter

La Semana (another Spanish-language newspaper)

Sam Pan (a bilingual monthly for the Chinese population)

Scandinavian Tribune

By listing all the newspapers in your area, as I have begun to do for Boston, you will start to develop a profile of available publicity outlets. In the future you will refer to this list frequently, selecting among the newspapers according to your needs. In Boston, both the *Globe* and the *Herald* would be targets of any publicity announcement. But because competition for their column space is usually less stiff, neighborhood weeklies, weeklies from nearby towns, and ethnic newspapers, if appropriate, should also be included. It is important to know your geographical region and not concentrate your publicity efforts in any single part of it. Get to know the people, too: after listing all the local papers, find copies and scan them. This will help you get an idea of the community's ethnic makeup and attitudes.

In addition to the dailies and weeklies in any city, appropriate wire services, magazines, and specialty publications should be placed on your media list. Many might be included in the Boston example, though possibilities are too numerous to list here. The number would depend, of course, on the subject of your publicity campaign.

Identifying Contacts

Determining the range of publications in your area is the first step in getting to know your local press. The second step involves identifying appropriate editors, reporters, and writers as newspaper contacts. This is particularly important when addressing large dailies, which may have several hundred employees. Sending two or three copies of a press release to a newspaper like the *Chicago Tribune* or the *Detroit Free Press* will not guarantee that the appropriate editors ever see it. You should take pains to identify editors and reporters by name and include those names on your media list. Large dailies are bureaucracies in themselves, with all types of bureaus, desks, sections, and editions that must be considered if your information is to be well placed. This is no small feat, but one well-placed release is worth a hundred sent randomly.

From a distance, most newspapers appear to be similarly organized. They all have corporate boards, publishers, editors-in-chief, executive editors, editors, managing editors, business managers, reporters, photographers, and so on. Although employees of different newspapers often have similar titles, their responsibilities and functions can differ considerably. The practical publicist should understand the major divisons of a large daily. There are commonly three: (1) the corporate board and executive committee, (2) the business division, and (3) the editorial division. The board consists of the chairman, the publisher, and other executive officers. They oversee the operation of the newspaper in its entirety; they should not, in most situations, be used as media contacts. The business division is another important part of a newspaper that has little to do with people who want to place publicity. It includes a business manager, accountants, a legal staff, advertising salesmen, the rest of the advertising department (which may include a subdivision for classified ads), circulation managers, general administrators such as payroll, promotion, and public relations directors (whose job it is to promote the newspaper, *not to help you promote your cause*).

The editorial division is the most important to the publicist. The *Washington Post*, the daily with the widest circulation in the nation's capital, lists these departments in its editorial division.

District News Desk (covers news originating from or concerning the District of Columbia)

Regional News Desk (covers news in the Middle Atlantic States)

Maryland/Virginia News Desk (concentrates on those two nearby states)

National News Desk

Editorial Page and Letters to the Editor

Book World and Literary Calendar

Business and Finance

Etcetera (prints personal opinion pieces by members of the general public—an important contact)

Fashion

Food

Obituaries

Ombudsman (receives complaints about news coverage and rectifies mistakes, often by having corrections printed)

Opinion Advertising (reviews paid advertisements that promote a viewpoint more than a product, such as those often placed by Mobil and the Moral Majority)

Outlook

Real Estate

Religion

Sports

Style

Travel

TV

Washington Business, Business Calendar, and News-makers (the latter section comprises features on business people in the news)

Washington Post Magazine

Weekend (presents articles on weekend entertainment)

Weekend's Best and Sporting Life (a calendar of activities)

Weekly, This Week (a calendar of upcoming events in the District of Columbia, many involving Congress)

Public Relations (supplies information to the public about *Post* services)

With a circulation of seven hundred thousand, the *Washington Post* is a large-scale newspaper. It has many sections, each with its own editor and writers. Although no other newspaper is organized quite like the *Post*, every large daily has its own special sections, which usually cover some of the topics listed here. By identifying the sections that relate to your publicity interests, and the editors and reporters for those sections, you can pinpoint important press contacts. This may involve a few telephone calls to get their names, of course. But the more specific you are in addressing your releases, the more effective your publicity will be.

A medium-sized newspaper, such as a weekly with a circulation of one hundred thousand, has a much smaller staff. For such a newspaper you would always include on your mailing list the news editor, assistant editor, feature

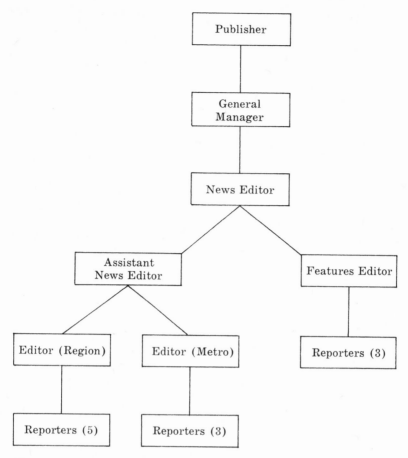

The generalized editorial structure of a medium-sized weekly, with a circulation of about one hundred thousand. The editors and reporters included here can all be used as publicity contacts. Efforts should be made, however, to identify precisely the beats or areas for which each editor and reporter is responsible.

editor, and perhaps one or two reporters who have covered topics similar to yours.

A smaller newspaper, such as a weekly with a circulation of five thousand or less, will probably have an even simpler editorial structure, with two or three key individuals. The news editor and the assistant editor, and perhaps a reporter, are important contacts for the publicist.

The editorial structures of magazines and specialty publications vary depending on size and circulation. For instance, a two-color, eight-page newsletter is probably the product of one editor-writer and maybe a graphic artist. A four-color glossy magazine with a circulation of fifty thousand, however, probably has a full complement of editors, writers, and artists. The editorial structure of magazines is usually more centralized than that of newspapers; since publication is less frequent, fewer people are needed to do the work.

Magazines often use free-lancers. Editors keep files on writers to call when appropriate stories come up and expect them to contact the magazine with their own story ideas. When you want to place some information in a magazine, contact the editor and the associate editor. (If you want to write a story yourself, especially, you should be sure to contact them before you begin.) Together they decide what stories will be covered and who will cover them; the editor,

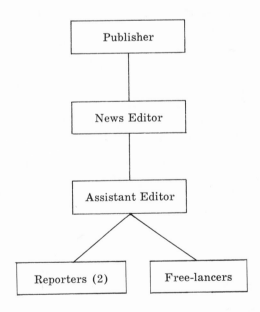

The generalized editorial structure of a small weekly, with a circulation of about five thousand.

in particular, must clear story ideas. You may want to include a writer or two on your mailing list, especially if they have shown interest in your subject or have written on related topics before.

The wire services, such as AP and UPI, are set up by bureaus. There is usually at least one bureau per state, and in major cities there is often more than one. A bureau chief, whose function is like that of an editor, assigns reporters to cover certain stories or beats. The local bureau chief should certainly be on your contact list, but because the reporters are encouraged to come up with stories on their own, you should take pains to identify contacts among them as well. In the larger bureaus there may be several editors who

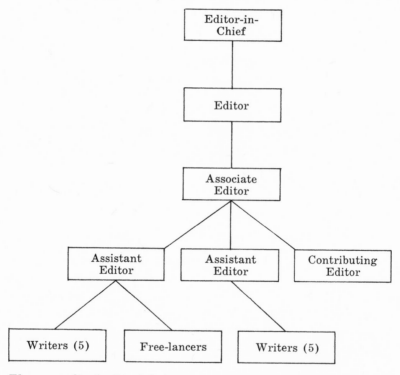

The generalized editorial structure of an average four-color magazine, with a circulation of about one hundred thousand. The editor and the associate editor usually determine what gets printed, so they are key publicity contacts. Other editors and writers, however, can also be reached with story ideas.

Name/Address	Type	Circulation	Editions	Deadlines	Contacts
Stafford Sun 121 Main St. Stafford, SD 252-8197	Daily	22,500	Mornings and Sunday	6:00 P.M.	Les Brown, news editor Wendy Baker, reporter
Buck County News 22 Longwood Ave. Rapahoe, SD 775-2100	Weekly	7,500	Tuesday afternoons	Thursdays 5:00 P.M.	Elizabeth Denison, news editor
The Outdoorsman 5 Center Rd. Bowie, SD 672-3363	Magazine	16,850	Monthly; first of month	Preceding month	Michael Day, editor Dwayne Moore, writer
The Winchester Suburban Triple Hill Center Winchester, SD 666-8775	Bimonthly newspaper	15,000	First and sixteenth of month	One week before publication	Leslie Appleworth, editor
UPI 440 Turnpike Ave. Stafford, SD 332-6500	Wire service	.....	Daily; no restrictions	Daily; no restrictions	Raymond Adams, bureau chief

Sample press chart. All information presented here has been invented.

cover feature stories, the state capitol, or economic news. You can find out their names and duties by calling the bureau for your region.

Once you have surveyed the press in your area and identified the appropriate editors and writers, it can be helpful to prepare a chart that lists the name of each publication or wire service, its address, contacts (editors and reporters), phone number, deadlines, circulation, and frequency of issue. As you develop more and more contacts you will find that it is hard to keep track of all these details. With a comprehensive chart to refer to, you will save time when you have to quickly select one or two publicity outlets among the many serving your area. Such a chart will also allow others in your organization to identify appropriate contacts in your absence.

4.

Words and Photos

THE most frequently used (and abused) method of publicizing an event in the newspaper is via the press release. The press release is the practical publicist's bread and butter, and you should be certain that you know the proper way to prepare one.

The Press Release

The standard format is simple. It is designed so your message will be readily and clearly understood by a busy editor, who must decide in minutes whether to run a press release as is or to assign a reporter to follow up the story. Most editors receive hundreds if not thousands of releases daily, and, as you might expect, most find their way into the trash basket.

Some releases do make it into print, however, and it is

usually their newsworthiness that determines the outcome. If you are announcing the outcome of a very controversial and highly publicized court case, a revolutionary break-through in finding a cure for cancer, or the resignation of a very high official, you can probably count on having your announcement printed. Unfortunately, most publicists don't have the advantage of announcing earth-shattering events. Big stories are usually first announced by reporters, who function much like the Richter scale; they record events, both big and small, as soon as they occur. The practical publicist, as a rule of thumb, should not try to compete with reporters but should concentrate on targeting select infor-mation to the right news people.

Most press releases announce routine events, such as the annual meeting of the local branch of the Audubon So-ciety or the birth of the first baby of the new year at the community hospital. Determining the newsworthiness of a press release is the editor's job. Nonetheless, if you are an-nouncing a very important event, a poorly prepared release can obscure your message and prevent an editor from recog-nizing its worth. If you have marginal news, moreover, the care you take in preparing your release can determine whether it gets put in print or in the circular file.

A press release can be anywhere from one to five pages in length, although one-page releases are preferred. Remem-ber, you are only trying to capture the attention of the edi-tor or reporter, not tell the story in full detail. Always use 8½-by-11-inch paper, preferably white, though a pale color is also acceptable. If you do not have letterhead, type the name and address of your organization at the top of the page, centered. Skip several lines, then type a contact's name and telephone number on the left-hand side of the page. Ed-itors will call the contact if they have questions or would like verification of details; it is important, therefore, to name someone who can be reached by phone easily and who is particularly knowledgeable about the subject of the re-lease as well as your organization. Make sure that the per-son who is named as contact knows it, and provide that per-son with a copy of the release. On the right-hand side of the page, on the same line as the contact's name, type FOR IMMEDIATE RELEASE and the mailing date, or FOR ADVANCE RELEASE ONLY with the earliest date on which the article should be printed.

Skip a few more lines and include a short, descriptive title—a one-line statement of the basic theme of the release. Newspapers rarely retain the titles that appear on press releases, so don't feel you should be witty, and don't get upset when an editor runs your release with a new title. Some publicists don't even include titles on their releases, and you shouldn't feel you have to. However, I like to use a well-focused title that will grab the editor's attention, if only for a second.

The body of the release should always be typed and double-spaced. Paragraphs should be short, five or six lines at maximum, in accordance with standard newspaper style. Set your margins so that each line on the page will be no longer than sixty characters, including spaces between words. This way the copy editor will have plenty of space for editorial marks, rewriting, and notes to the printer. If you use a second page, type the word *more* at the bottom of the first, centered. At the top of the second page type the title of the release again, centered, and add the word *continued* in parentheses. Releases vary considerably in content, but with practice the beginning publicist will no doubt become confident with the short form, no matter what the topic. There are a few guidelines that should be followed in the meantime.

Try to include the name of an official, or well-known and well-respected person, as I've done at the start of the sample release with the name of Commissioner Pac. Immediately you will convey a sense of importance to the editor. If no "big name" is associated with your organization, quote your president or executive director and identify his or her station to add authority (for example, "Peter Period, president of the Grammarian's Guild, announced . . ."). The timeliness of your release should be apparent from the lead paragraph; point out that the official announcement was made today or yesterday. Or, in the case of an advance re-

STATE OF CONNECTICUT
DEPARTMENT OF ENVIRONMENTAL PROTECTION

COASTAL AREA MANAGEMENT PROGRAM

* * * PRESS RELEASE * * * * * * PRESS RELEASE * * *

FOR FURTHER INFORMATION: FOR IMMEDIATE RELEASE:
David Tedone (203) 566-7404   June 10, 1981

STATE FUNDS SILVER SANDS, MILFORD

Commissioner Stanley Pac, Department of Environmental Protection (DEP), announced today that $15,000 will be allocated to the city of Milford this summer to keep Silver Sands State Park open to the public. "The $15,000 will be taken from the State's Coastal Management Grant and will go to assist the city of Milford in maintaining Silver Sands State Park with respect to lifeguards, trash pickup, and police protection," Pac said. Although the site is owned by the state, the city has generally assumed responsibility for maintenance of the park.

Early last week Milford Mayor Henry Povinelli had promised that if "Pac came up with $10,000, I'd put our crews in there to clean the beaches and Recreation Director Ed Austin could put in some lifeguards."

By Memorial Day Silver Sands had already hosted large crowds of sunbathers, and the amount of trash left scattered caused residents to complain about the lack of maintenance. Mayor Povinelli admitted at the time that "there is no money to maintain the area despite the responsibility."

Silver Sands has been the subject of controversy for several years.

- more -

Phone: (203) 566-7404
71 Capitol Avenue ● Hartford, Connecticut 06115
An Equal Opportunity Employer

Silver Sands Park (continued)

Originally, the state acquired the property under an agreement to develop and maintain the site as a park. However, full responsibility for the property will not be transferred to the state until 1984, and efforts by the state to build a highway connector to the beach have given some Milford residents second thoughts.

"Given the shortage of sandy beach in Connecticut and the intense demand for summer recreation," Pac said, "it would be morally irresponsible not to do all we could to keep the 290-acre area from being placed off limits. I am pleased to announce that through the State's Coastal Management Program Grant, citizens will be able to enjoy the beach in Milford this summer."

Arthur Rocque, director of DEP's Planning and Coastal Management Program, added that the state "was happy to have the opportunity to secure special funds from the federal government for this purpose. Unfortunately," he warned, "the $15,000 is a one-time, special grant, and hopefully the state legislature will be able to come up with the money to further maintain Silver Sands next year."

The state has had strong financial backing for its park system in the past. Officials estimate that development of Silver Sands will cost more than $20 million, more than $4 million of which has already been invested in the site. While more than $16 million has been lined up by the DEP from federal and state sources, recent budget cuts appear to jeopardize these funds.

- 30 -

Sample press release. (Courtesy Connecticut Coastal Area Management Program.)

lease, say something like: "Peter Period will announce on Friday. . . ." Once you have gotten through the routine preliminaries you should make a summary statement, explaining as succinctly as possible your main purpose for issuing the release. In the sample the summary statement is: "$15,000 will be allocated to the city of Milford this summer to keep Silver Sands open to the public." With this information the editor doesn't have to read the whole release to find out what's going on but is able to determine immediately whether the subject is newsworthy or not.

The rest of the release should elaborate on the summary statement; this is the key to developing a good press release. Each paragraph following the main paragraph should add clarifying details. The paragraphs should progressively become less important; once again, the editor should get the most important news first. If the available column space can accommodate only half the release, moreover, the editor can easily slash away the last three paragraphs.

The editor's job will be much easier if each paragraph functions as a distinct unit while relating details concerning the main subject. The editor then decides, given the newspaper's column restraints, how much to tell the audience, and he or she can take out a couple of middle paragraphs, if necessary, without worrying about losing an important detail. Often editors will make substantive as well as stylistic changes. They may rewrite sentences and even whole paragraphs, including the all-important lead paragraph. Unless a crucial error is made, you shouldn't become upset if you find your release substantially altered. Publicists seldom see one of their press releases printed word for word. Remember, your first objective is to get the editor's attention; second, to have him print part or all of your release, in any form; and third, to have him assign a reporter to do follow-up stories.

Editors frequently change press releases to "localize" them—to tell how a government decision, for instance, will affect their town or nearby towns. This is especially likely to happen if you are working on a national campaign, and the events you are describing affect many communities or regions of the country. Editors may follow up your release by contacting the individuals named or by adding quotes and information that they have gathered from other sources.

Include quotes in your release whenever practical. Direct quotes from key people tell the story more effectively than paraphrase or straight third-person exposition. They fit in naturally when you are relating an official announcement; they convey veracity, immediacy, and newsworthiness. You should avoid putting in too many quotes—just select two or three snappy ones that best underscore your message. At the very least, including quotes in a release allows the editor or reporter to abstract the quotes and write a new article from them. In essence, you are acting as the eyes and ears of the newspaper; you are the one on the scene.

To end your press release, always skip two lines and center one of the following symbols: crosshatch (#), the number thirty (–30–), or simply "End." All of these symbols are generally acceptable, and their meaning is clearly recognized.

Many press releases simply announce an upcoming event, performance, or meeting; these are called spot releases. They are simple to issue, so long as the standard format is utilized. Simply ask yourself who, what, where, when, and why (that is, why is this news? With performances you should also ask how much). Suppose you arrived at the following answers:

WHO: The Merrymakers Acting Guild

WHAT: A performance of Edward Albee's
           Who's Afraid of Virginia Woolf?

WHERE: The Pildown Club Auditorium, 850 Main
           Street, Sawtucket, Rhode Island

WHEN: Friday, September 4, 1982, at 8:00 P.M.

WHY: The fourth and final performance of their
           1982 season

HOW MUCH: One dollar general admission

Sample spot release.

The press release on this performance should be short
and sweet. You would thus tell the newspapers what they
need to know in the sparest of terms. The editor can tell at
a glance what is going on (who, what, where, why, when,
and how much). Your announcement will probably be included in the arts section or weekend section, which usually
runs on Fridays in a daily—just in time for the performance. A spot release should be issued very close to curtain

time, when its news value is greatest, and sent to all local papers.

You can enhance your publicity efforts by using what I call the double-barreled press release. Although your spot release will be issued immediately before the performance, prepare it early. From it develop a more detailed release that will attract the editor's interest—and the public's. Mail the longer release well in advance of the planned event. Compare the expanded release on the Merrymakers' performance to the spot release on the same subject.

The announcement for the "gala performance" includes more information than the spot release. By mentioning the celebration of the tenth successful season and the wine and cheese party, you heighten the release's appeal and increase its news value, for you are heralding rare occasions that merit public attention. The artistic director's remarks add drama—he is a person of authority making a special statement. The basic information about the performance—who, what, where, when, why, and how much—is contained in the second paragraph. The three remaining paragraphs elaborate on the first. They provide interesting details about the guild's history, financing, and celebration of success. The press release thus focuses on two common human interests: finances and success.

You should issue an expanded release two weeks before the event, so that newspapers will have plenty of time to run it or perhaps write a full story on the subject. Even if the editors do not assign a reporter to the story but simply print your release as is, you will have succeeded in getting the public's attention. Remember, your first objective is to get an editor's attention (and thereby the readers') ; your second objective is to get your message across. After you have managed to place your expanded release, be sure to send the spot release as a reminder just before the performance.

Using photographs. Press releases can be effectively punctuated with photographs. A high-quality photo of your subject or speaker is an excellent attention-getting device. When you pick up a newspaper, your eye is attracted by photos

The Merrymakers Acting Guild

100 Prospect Street • Sawtucket, Rhode Island 05019

* * * PRESS RELEASE * * *   * * * PRESS RELEASE * * *

FOR FURTHER INFORMATION: FOR IMMEDIATE RELEASE:
Audrey Amplification 277-7575   August 18, 1982

MERRYMAKERS' GALA PERFORMANCE

Dick Ostrea, Artistic Director for the Merrymakers' Acting Guild, announced today that the performance of Edward Albee's Who's Afraid of Virginia Woolf? will mark the conclusion of the Guild's tenth season. "We are going to wind up our most successful season with a sizzling performance and a wine-and-cheese party for the audience." he said.

Originally staged in 1964, Who's Afraid of Virginia Woolf? won top drama awards and was later made into a movie starring Elizabeth Taylor and Richard Burton. The Merrymakers' performance will be held on Friday, September 4, 1982, at 8:00 P.M., Pildown Club Auditorium, 850 Main Street, Sawtucket. General admission is $1.00. The Guild performance stars Hermine Adams, Daniel Black, Dana McAndrews, and Phelps Dodge.

- more -

"GALA PERFORMANCE" (continued)

To mark the Guild's tenth successful season, the audience and patrons will be invited to a free wine-and-cheese party after the performance in the lobby, where they can meet and talk with the cast and production crew.

"Receipts over the past five years have more than tripled," Mr. Ostrea revealed, "placing this season's performances soundly in the black." Mr. Ostrea also commented that the success of the Guild is "proof that residents of Sawtucket county recognize and appreciate good theater."

The Merrymakers Acting Guild was established in 1972 to foster the performing arts in Sawtucket. The Guild grew rapidly during the seventies, although funds came solely from membership and ticket sales. In 1975 Mr. Ostrea became Artistic Director. With financial backing from the Sawtucket Savings and Loan Association and the National Endowment for the Arts, the Guild has blossomed into a full-fledged acting company offering four performances each season. This year's works included plays by Ionesco, Pirandello, Miller, and Albee.

- End -

Expanded press release.

Soprano Janice Giampa will perform Francis Poulenc's "La Voix Humaine," a lyric tragedy in one act, tonight at 8:00 at the French Library, 53 Marlborough Street, Boston. Tickets are $2.50 for members and students and $3.50 for nonmembers. A wine and cheese reception will follow the concert. Call 266-4354 for details.

and headlines; first you look at these, then you begin to read. Photos work particularly well with short press releases, such as the Merrymakers spot announcement. When editors receive such an announcement with a photo, they will often print the photo and include the who, what, where, and so on, as a caption. Photographs of performers, such as the one of soprano Janice Giampa, can be very effective.

Although the captioned information had been prepared in the standard press release format, the editor chose to emphasize the photograph rather than the text; thus, it wasn't even necessary to include a headline. The composition of the photograph is simple yet effective. Ms. Giampa's face fills the frame, creating a sense of intimacy and demanding the reader's attention. By excluding extraneous details, you ensure that your subject will not be obscured through poor newspaper reproduction.

Landscape scenes also work well with press releases. A photo of Silver Sands Beach could well accompany the press release announcing the $15,000 award to the city of Milford, Connecticut. It really doesn't matter which season the photo is taken in, though summertime with people sunbathing tends to capture the mood or theme, and perhaps shots of trash barrels overflowing, or a barricade and sign saying "off limits" would even be more dramatic. But don't get too fancy.

When taking photos of people, you should avoid giving the impression that your subject has been posed. To ensure a natural appearance, engage your subjects in conversation. Ask questions, and as they respond they will inevitably gesture and assume a typical stance or pose, making your photo appear as if it were taken during the subject's normal activities. Strive for photos that are believable by helping your subject to relax.

Because many press releases are announcements of people making announcements, you will often be expected to provide photos of your speakers before small crowds, at desks, or behind microphones. Shoot several pictures of your subjects as they speak. Try to capture your speakers in characteristic poses, when they *look* as if they are making announcements or answering questions.

In photographing a group, such as a musical band, you may have to pose your subjects yourself. You can overcome

A photo of a beach scene such as this might accompany the Silver Sands press release.

Two photos of Muhammad Ali. At left, a formal portrait; at right, a shot of the champ in action, talking to reporters. The action shot makes a more interesting publicity photo. (Courtesy Fay Foto, Boston.)

the drabness of an artificial arrangement, however, by making it distinctive.

Striking poses, historic feats or events, and familiar faces are naturals for press photos. Examples are the high school high jumper hurling himself over the cross bar, the governor turning a shovelful of dirt to start excavation for the new hospital, or Marilyn Monroe. Sometimes a little imagination can do wonders with an otherwise mundane subject. This is particularly true with inanimate objects— we've all seen ads displaying cars on top of magnificent Western mountains. The quickest way to get a feeling for dramatic photography is to examine almost any glossy magazine. Advertisers have been using tricks to attract attention to mundane subjects for generations. But always guard against getting too fancy.

My recommendations on picture taking are intended as guidelines only—you need not follow them religiously. Photography can be a high art, and there are few limits to the beauty and interest that a talented photographer can evoke from almost any subject. Examine the photos in any newspaper for ideas and inspiration. Whenever possible, employ an experienced photographer for your publicity shots.

When including a photograph with your press release, you should send a glossy black and white print, at least 5 inches by 7 inches in size. Choose those prints that are in sharp focus, with plenty of contrast—you don't want a picture that has mostly gray tones, because it will lose clarity when printed in a newspaper. A marginally good photo will look terrible on newsprint. Magazines, with their glossy paper and color printing, can handle a much broader range of photos—whether prints, slides, or transparencies—than newspapers can. But because they need months of lead time, most magazines are poor outlets for items of immediate importance. But if your announcements do not have time restrictions, then by all means send them to magazines, and include appropriate photos.

Never write on the back of a photograph; if you do, an impression will almost surely show on the front. Instead,

In good publicity photos, speakers look as if they are interacting with their audiences. Here Henry Kissinger listens thoughtfully to questions from reporters. (Courtesy Fay Foto, Boston.)

Photographing large groups can be difficult. This shot is effective because the subjects have assumed natural poses and are all looking at the camera, engaging the viewer's attention. (Courtesy Art Department, University of Connecticut.)

write all essential information—suggested caption and identification of subject—on a piece of paper. Tape the paper to the back of the photo at the bottom edge, so your words will show below. Needless to say, you should never bend, staple, or paper-clip a photograph.

Never draw crop marks directly on a photo, and never crop by cutting off unwanted areas of the photograph. To indicate what part of a photo should be reproduced, simply tape a sheet of tissue paper to the back with masking tape, fold the tissue over the face of the photo so it is completely covered, and draw the crop marks on the tissue paper. Any printer will be able to determine the desired size. (Keep in mind that newspapers may crop your photo again—perhaps more than you'd like.)

When mailing a photo with a press release, be sure to enclose it in two pieces of corrugated cardboard, and write on the envelope "Photo enclosed." The postal service can easily damage a photograph that is mailed without such protection.

As you decide where you should mail your press release

and photograph, keep in mind that the cost of photographic prints becomes less as you order more. For instance, an eight-by-ten-inch glossy black and white print usually costs about two dollars; each additional copy costs between 25 and 50 cents.

The Press Kit

This is another important item in the practical publicist's repertoire. A collection of informative materials designed to brief reporters and editors on a project, the press kit is sent to potentially interested members of the press before a media campaign begins. It provides background information on your organization and on the campaign you are undertaking, and it identifies key persons and how to reach them. Your kit should provide members of the press with everything they need to conduct an interview and write a story.

Assemble your press kit *after* you have completed your

Action adds interest to otherwise boring photos. This shot of a park is brought to life by the people using it. Though the park may be the subject of the press release, it becomes a setting in the accompanying publicity photo. (Courtesy Jewish Big Brother and Fay Foto, Boston.)

program planning. Its contents should be chosen carefully to provide leads for reporters. Emphasize the people involved; reporters always look for the human-interest angle. Your writing should always be direct and sincere; otherwise, you may be the subject of a not-so-flattering report.

The contents of a press kit may vary considerably depending on the project. For example, suppose your community has recently formed a group to combat rape. If you want to draw the public's attention to the problem of rape and your efforts to control it, you will be wise to introduce yourself to local papers by means of a press kit. The kit should include a "fact sheet" containing a statement of your group's purpose, a count of your members, and a list of officers (especially if they are well-known and respected members of the community), and some statistics on rape in your area. You will also want to provide supporting information in your press kit. This may include a transcript of your president's recent speech on rape and its effects on the community, a brochure on rape published by the state health department or the federal Department of Health and Human Services, and a handbill describing how women can avoid encounters with rapists and what they should do if they are attacked. You should include an outline of your strategy for combating the problem, and a calendar of future events—upcoming meetings of your group, special presentations on the subject, and community meetings in which your members will participate. This will enable reporters and editors to prepare their schedules for covering future events.

If later you must cancel a meeting listed in your calendar, be sure to notify all reporters and editors who have received your press kit. Reporters are impressed by efficient community organizations, and nothing will turn them away faster than failure to hold scheduled meetings. Efficiency and reliability establish credibility, and credibility is important in dealing with the press.

The packaging of a press kit is also very important. Remember, it is the first contact a reporter or editor will have with your group. You want to make your kit neat,

Parents for Sex Education

One High Street • Practicality, Missouri 63069

Evelyn Markey
President

Jane Widmark
Treasurer

John Sperio, Ph.D.
Secretary

4,500 members

THE FACTS ON SEX EDUCATION

FACT: Sex education for children is a controversial social issue. Unfortunately, many political and community leaders react to the issue without considering the facts.

FACT: When asked to identify the most important sources of information on sex, students rate their peers first, and the mass media second. Needless to say, many of their peers are misinformed, and information communicated by the media can be easily misunderstood.

FACT: Each day our children are exposed to dozens of sexual messages from TV, movies, magazines, pop music, and advertisements. In many cases, those messages are inane and exploitative.

FACT: Nationally, only 10 percent of all students receive a comprehensive sex education course. Only New Jersey, Maryland, and Kentucky require sex education courses.

FACT: Opinion polls have shown that 80 percent of all parents want sex education in schools.

FACT: Surveys have shown that sex education does not encourage sexual activity among teenagers.

FACT: The real issue of sex education is not whether or not to offer sex education in the schools, but where and how it should be taught.

FACT: Parents for Sex Education (PSE) is sponsoring a campaign to promote sex education in local schools. If you want to help, call 222-1123.

Sample fact sheet.

handy, and attractive; all written materials must be interesting and easy to read. The least expensive way to package a press kit is with a simple folder made of card stock, with two pockets on the inside to hold loose papers. Your contacts can use the folder as a ready-made file as they receive future materials from you. Place any booklets and general information on your group in the left-hand pocket. Your fact sheet and other materials relating specifically to your campaign should be placed in the right-hand pocket. Be sure that your materials fit neatly into the pockets; don't overload them so they tear, and don't underload them so that the papers easily slide out. Have everything printed or photocopied on bond paper. If you can afford them, a selection of light-colored papers can help individuate your materials.

Of everything in the kit, the fact sheet is probably the most important. Since it is the first item that you would like the reporter to read, place the fact sheet (labeled such in large letters) in the right-hand pocket at the front, with the other materials behind it in order of importance.

Write a cover letter on your organization's letterhead and paper-clip it to the front of the folder. Your letter should introduce your group and describe exactly what the kit contains. If you address reporters and editors personally in the heading of the letter, they will be more likely to read it.

To whom do you mail the press kit? To as many key media people as possible. Their names and addresses will make up your basic mailing list for future press releases and news flashes.

Monitoring Press Coverage

Once you have established contacts through your press kits and press releases, you should continue to monitor the newspapers. Those that carry your stories or print your releases should be followed closely. When reporters unknown to you write on the topic of your concern, you might call to offer congratulations on a "thoughtful" or "worthwhile" article as a way of identifying yourself with the issue. You might offer them further information, as well, and remind them of an upcoming event. Suggest that they stop by your group's office sometime, or attend your next regular meeting, so that they can meet some of your officers and key members. If a reporter has not heard of your group, send a press kit or other materials and place the reporter's name on your mailing list. One note of caution: be helpful and available, but never be overly solicitous. Reporters like to establish as many contacts as possible, but they tend to shy away when they suspect ulterior motives. And many are very aware of the publicity game. Take pains to establish direct personal contact, but be tactful.

If a story about your group contains a flagrant error, call the reporter and point it out. You should, however, exercise the utmost caution and tact when confronting a reporter in this manner. Never call when you are angry—no matter how angry a report makes you—or you may say things you will regret later. Instead of challenging reporters, try to win them over so that the damage doesn't recur. Refrain from making a blanket statement to the effect that the article is totally incorrect. Instead, say that you found the article disturbing because it is unbalanced, it does not reflect the whole picture, or it lacks some basic information. Be ready to point out specific inaccuracies and suggest how they can be clarified. In many instances you will find that the reporter used inadequate sources, misunderstood the issues, or interviewed only persons with similar viewpoints. If you demonstrate open-mindedness—by making it clear that you are calling not to retaliate but to set the record straight—then the reporter will usually be receptive. Most writers, you can assume, are sensitive about their work, so your criticism should be gentle. I usually like to end the conversation by suggesting a few knowledgeable people the reporter could talk to for perspective, and I even offer their phone numbers. If you do not seem to be making any headway, you can try talking to the editor in charge or, if that fails, the newspaper's ombudsman.

The Newspaper Interview

Most people think that all reporters are like Mike Wallace on "60 Minutes"—aggressively and relentlessly trying to catch people contradicting themselves. This is a misconception. Most reporters are not investigative, and investigative reporters usually cover illicit activities or the government. You can probably bet that a local reporter covering the Merrymakers Acting Guild, the High Plains Rape Crisis Center, or any other community-based organization is not doing so to discredit your group. And I would seriously doubt that such a reporter could harbor suspicions concerning kickbacks and bribes. So unless you have something to hide, relax; put these stereotypes out of mind.

You can take any of several tacks when being interviewed, depending on the circumstances. Some basic guidelines, however, can help you create a positive impression and communicate your ideas effectively. When reporters ask you for an interview, try to find out what they want; don't assume anything. What kind of article are they looking for, a news story or a feature? Have they talked to anyone else? When will the story be appearing?

You should try to find out if your interview is going to make up the entire story, or if other people will be interviewed. Reporters like to balance interviewees against each other, to present both the pros and the cons. Sometimes reporters will do a broad story, say, on the Equal Rights Amendment. They will conduct several major interviews and flesh out the story by interviewing marginally related people, such as the director of the High Plains Rape Crisis Center. As a result, the reporter may use only one quote from your director, and the quote may have little to do with the problem of rape. It is up to a good publicist to figure out the reporter's angle and make sure comments are tailored to the organization's best advantage.

Once you know what the reporter's focus will be, set a time and place for the interview. Identify the interviewee (if not yourself) and describe that person's background briefly. Reporters like to move fast; if they call for an interview they may expect to meet you that day—in an hour, perhaps—or even interview you over the phone. Don't be afraid to put them off a day or two. This is a good practice because it allows you time to prepare. Often reporters protest, "But I have to meet today's deadline!" And often they do. If their deadline is near, offer to call them back in one hour—and make sure you do. In an hour's time you can anticipate questions and write down a few concise statements.

Before reporters arrive, scan the newspaper they represent to see if you can find any articles they have written. If they plan to interview your director, arrange to meet them yourself first. The meeting place should be comfortable and quiet. A private office is usually best, although reporters sometimes like to meet in neutral territory, such as at a local restaurant, coffee shop, or bar. Such surroundings help the interviewee to relax and become reflective. Remember that the setting may be mentioned in the story, and that it may color your interview. Don't meet in a seedy bar or restaurant with a bad reputation. A room with books will help you appear serious, but you might choose an informal setting that reflects your concerns. If you are talking about a basketball team, meet on a court or in the locker room. A meeting with Dick Ostrea, the flamboyant artistic director of the Merrymakers Acting Guild, might be scheduled to occur backstage, or even on the empty stage immediately following a rehearsal. The dramatic setting will aid the reporter in writing an interesting story.

Perhaps the best way to prepare for the interview itself is to write out a list of anticipated questions, such as "What is the overall goal of the Wedgewood Croquet Club?" or "How would you characterize the community's response to the problem of battered women?" or "What would you say to someone who totally opposed equal rights for blacks?" Such questions help you to start thinking broadly and objectively—to regain the perspective you tend to lose working for a group day in and day out. Prepare your answers concisely yet completely.

Anticipate questions for which the answers seem obvious—even reporters who are very familiar with your organization may ask, "So tell me, how did the 'Guardian Angels' come about?" They may know exactly how the Guardian Angels came about, but they ask the question to get a quote from you. Your general, unambiguous reply will provide background for their readers. Above all, be direct and honest. Avoid rambling; answer each question separately and thoroughly, as you would if you were approached by a stranger asking for directions.

If you don't know how to answer a question, or if you are unsure of the answer, simply say so. Tell the reporter you will think about it or ask someone, and call later with a response.

Before the interview, refresh your memory concerning your group by rereading background information or handouts such as a fact sheet. Then make a list of statements you would like to make. Once again, actually write your statements down; it helps you to express yourself clearly during the interview. Have facts and figures (like date of inception, numbers of members) handy. Reporters like details. If you make a statement concerning "a lot of money" the reporter will probe:

REPORTER: How much money?

INTERVIEWEE (wanting to remain vague): A lot of money.

REPORTER: Is it more than $10,000? Is it less than $1,000?

Get the picture? Avoid being vague.

At times you will run into reporters who like to play devil's advocate. They will ask probing questions, usually preceded by "What if . . . ?" Reporters' interviewing techniques vary; some like to get you mad or excited, whereas others try to make you feel threatened. They ask emotionally charged questions to provoke an unexpected response—a pithy quote or two. Learn to stay calm and unruffled, no matter how pointed the questions seem. Your matter-of-fact style will defuse a potentially hostile reporter. Nine times out of ten you will know more about the issues than the reporter, so don't be afraid to take charge of an interview.

Getting your picture taken. The newspaper that sends a reporter to interview you will probably also want your photo. On small, local newspapers the reporters themselves sometimes take the photos. If such is the case, then a photogenic room—one with a fireplace, for example—is a good place for the interview. Professional photographers usually arrive a day or two after the interview, except in the case of a late-breaking story.

Remember that your image is very important; you want your photo to attract attention and add weight to your interview. I once interviewed the president of an oyster company in his home on a rainy winter day. When I had written up my story, the magazine that accepted it dispatched a photographer to meet the president at a wharf, where he was photographed in his element—against the background of the sea. Your photograph needn't express your concerns so conspicuously. However, you don't want to look foolish, either, by appearing in an ironic setting. You can usually manipulate your setting somewhat, and you can always create a serious image by having your photo snapped before a wall of books. Books add weight to your words, which is why politicians like to have their pictures taken in rooms full of them.

Writing Articles and Letters to the Editor

There are two more good methods for breaking into print in your local weekly or daily. Writing articles on a free-lance basis can assure newspaper coverage of your cause. But free-lance writing is time-consuming and difficult; appropriate writing skills are necessary. Writing an article doesn't guarantee that a newspaper will print it, either; you may submit a piece only to learn that the editor is uninterested. If you do elect to write a few articles—or have an experienced writer write them for you—make sure that the topic is cleared with the appropriate editor first. If they have never worked with you before, editors may express interest in your topic and your approach but reserve acceptance until they see your finished manuscript. For the beginning publicist, free-lance articles should not be a high priority, unless you have several volunteer writers who can work on articles while you run the rest of the media campaign.

One form of writing that should not be overlooked is letters to the editor. Most publications print letters from their readers. You can occasionally call the public's attention to a subject or take issue with an article previously published by addressing a letter to your newspaper's editor. Such letters are typically between one and three pages in length. Always sign them with your name, your president's name, and the name of your group. Breaking into print, through a letter to the editor or a front-page story, helps to establish credibility and a public identity—an ultimate goal of the practical publicist.

5.

Soft Messages from Radio

HAVING your message broadcast on the radio may, on first thought, seem like an expensive way to generate publicity for your local group. But there are simple and inexpensive ways to reach both broad and select segments of the populace via radio. Despite the growth of television, radio has grown in importance as a community medium, relating local news and events in a compelling fashion. Ten seconds of radio broadcast time can have very favorable effects on a publicity campaign. Along with television, radio has taken over much of the function of the evening newspaper, and evening news broadcasts have in turn given immediacy to local affairs—whether the subject is voter registration, water pollution, local ballet, or high school soccer.

Radio is an intimate medium: it is far less intrusive than television and requires less concentration than newspapers. Radio is portable; you can listen to it while doing almost anything else. Publicists call radio the summer medium; when outdoor activities increase and television viewing drops off, people take their radios to the beach and to the mountains. They listen while they drive, and they listen while they play. Today, the revolution in microelectronics has made radio more intimate and more portable than ever. Coupled with headphones, radios are worn by joggers, subway riders, and roller skaters. As a subtle, companionable medium, radio is a powerful persuader. Daytime radio is more influential than daytime television, because far more people can listen to radio than can watch television while they work.

As a publicist you can take advantage of opportunities for free publicity offered by local radio stations if you understand the way radio stations operate. If you are wondering why radio stations run public service programs when most people would prefer to hear music, you may be surprised to learn that they are required by law to do so. In order to use public air waves, a radio station must be licensed by the Federal Communications Commission (FCC) of the federal government. In order to maintain its license, the station must serve its community by providing air time for nonprofit public interest groups, as well as political, educational, and public affairs programs, and editorial remarks and citizen comments. Although competition for time on a local station can be stiff, practical (and sometimes poor) publicists have a right, protected by law, to express themselves over the radio.

The first step to take in planning radio publicity is to identify the stations serving your area. A single community may have several radio stations, depending on the size of the local population. To stay in business, each station must reach a specific segment of the population, although there is some overlap between stations. The typical middle-sized city may have stations that feature news; talk shows; rock, jazz, classical, or top-forty music; ethnic programming; or even public affairs. Some stations may broadcast primarily in a foreign language, such as Spanish, Greek, or Armenian. Determine the specialties and types of audience for every station in your area. A station that plays mostly rock music, for instance, probably has a young, teenaged audience; therefore, announcements concerning the elderly would not be well placed on such a station.

The type of audience a radio station attracts, and the size of that audience, is partly determined by its mode of transmission, either AM (Amplitude Modulation) or FM (Frequency Modulation). AM transmissions usually reach a larger audience because the waves literally bounce off buildings, hills, mountains, and even clouds. FM transmissions are limited because they travel in a line of sight. If you are to hear an FM broadcast, there must be minimal interference from buildings and the like between your receiver and the station's transmitting antenna. FM broadcasters, therefore, are at a disadvantage in trying to reach the largest audiences, which are usually clustered in cities, but their transmissions tend to be clearer, with less static, than those of AM stations.

The amount of watts that a radio station produces also limits the size of the potential audience. The largest stations produce some fifty thousand watts, and on a clear day (or, usually, night, since there is normally less interference after dark) broadcasts can reach across several states. The smallest stations produce about 150 to 200 watts; their broadcasts are usually restricted to a single community.

If you were to survey a city the size of Dallas, Texas you would find about thirty radio stations. By calling them or looking them up in a directory such as *Broadcasting Yearbook* (see the last chapter of this book), you would find that they have different frequencies, channels, formats, network affiliates, broadcasting times, programming, and audiences. Some of the thirty stations in Dallas are FM, the others AM. Their programming also varies; some play "adult contemporary music," others religious and inspirational music, rock, country western, jazz, black gospel, or classical music. Some concentrate on programs of interest to blacks; others run news and talk shows; and still others broadcast educational programs. By determining the size of each station's audience and its style of programming, you

can pretty much target your news releases and PSAs to select groups. If you were publicizing the Dallas Symphony,
for instance, you would make sure that WRR (FM), the
classical music station, received all your calendar listings,
news releases, PSAs, and other announcements. If you were
working with the local hospital on a sickle cell anemia program, a disease that mainly affects blacks, then your announcements would be well-placed on KSKY (AM), the
black gospel station, and on KNON (FM), a station that
offers twelve hours of special programming for blacks each
day. Of course, you would make sure that your announcements concerning the sickle cell anemia clinic were to be
aired during these twelve hours.

Identifying Radio Contacts

Radio stations have small staffs in comparison to large
newspapers or local television stations. As a publicist, you
are interested in the program director, who decides what
shows are produced; the news director, who decides what
news should be covered and broadcast; the reporters, who
report on the news (and who are often looking for leads),
and the public affairs director, who coordinates PSAs and
other public services. Because specificity is the key to effectively placing publicity spots on local radio, you should ana-
lyze the organizational structure of each station you plan to
work with and identify each staff member by name and
function. Some of the smaller stations may have one person
directing all news and public affairs broadcasting. Occasionally one person will have dual functions; for example, a reporter may also be the public affairs director.

You can make a chart of radio contacts just as you
made one of press contacts. You should note the station
identification code, address, phone number, and, most im-
portantly, specific contacts. Note whether the station is AM
or FM, the types of programs it offers, the size of the audience, and broadcast times. Identify the station as independent commercial (if it sells advertising), public (if it is
supported by grants or by donations from its listeners), or

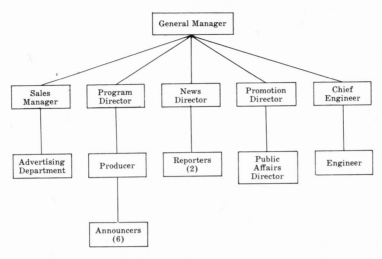

The generalized organization of a radio station. Individual stations vary considerably in structure, depending on the size and programming of each. The publicist should identify persons in the offices shown here, however, and should maintain contact with the news director and individual reporters as well as the promotion director and public affairs director.

a network affiliate (ABC, NBC, or CBS). In the case of a network affiliate, the network supplies national news programs, which the station usually supplements with a local news show. List the public services available (you can best find out by phoning the station): talk shows, PSAs, public affairs programs, call-in shows, or a community calendar. Each one of these public services can be utilized by the practical and radio-wise publicist.

Your radio contacts should receive any press releases, media kits, letters, or announcements that you would normally send a newspaper contact. Press releases remind them that your group is still around and update them on your activities. Sometimes the news director will respond to a release by sending a reporter to cover a meeting or event. Other times reporters will take a few quotes from your press release and build a story around it for broadcast; they may phone you for a quote or two. Like press reporters, radio reporters like to develop sources and contacts, so try

Station	AM or FM/Affiliate	Format	PSAs	Public Service Programs	News	Contacts
KJNF 961 Skopes Rd. Portland, OR 332-3567	FM 94.8 Independent	Classical, music of the forties	10, 20 secs.	Community calendar Citizen editorials	8:00 A.M. 9:00 A.M. 12:00 P.M. 6:00 P.M. 11:00 P.M.	Blaine Ready, news Jenny Hinds, public affairs Herb Wright, editorials
KGHB 101 Laugh Lane Salem, OR 672-1234	FM 90.2 Independent	Rock, ethnic	10, 30, 60 secs.	Community calendar	5:00 P.M.	Jerry Walters, news Toni Livery, public affairs
KKNC 85 Drury St. Salem, OR 672-9500	AM 1410 Independent	Top forty, contemporary, ethnic	30, 60 secs.	Commentary Art reviews Outdoor features	Hourly	Bill Trini, news Jane Allen, news Wally Treble, public affairs Mike McWilliams, commentary
KWAX 6 East Ave. Portland, OR 881-6666	AM 1260 CBS	News	10, 20 secs.	Citizen editorials Community features Newsmakers	All day	Frank D'Onato, news Jean Hart, public affairs Lewis Luckinbill, editorials Ray Handley, features Drew Lewis, Newsmakers
KPOP 1551 E. Main St. Portland, OR 882-4124	AM 840 NBC	Contemporary, jazz	10, 30 secs.	Community calendar Current event features Musician interviews	10:00 A.M. 12:00 P.M. 2:00 P.M. 6:00 P.M.	Louise Chamblis, news Jay Harrison, public affairs Janice Wonderton, features Harry Tones, interviews

Sample radio chart. All information presented here has been invented.

to cultivate relationships with them. Through these relationships you can build an image for your group of reliability, accuracy, and credibility.

The Radio PSA

Aside from the standard news release, the easiest and most cost-effective way to get your message on the radio is through the public service announcement (PSA). PSAs are rather like press releases, only they are much briefer, and they are heard rather than read by the audience. Practically all radio stations offer time for PSAs, which range from ten to sixty seconds in length. Ten seconds may seem like a short time, but in contrast with a newspaper article—of which many people read only the first sentence or paragraph—ten seconds of radio publicity can help your cause a lot. Besides, effective publicity is often a game of seconds. If an announcement is prepared correctly, ten seconds may be all you need to get your point across.

As a rule of thumb for determining the reading time of a PSA, figure ten seconds for every twenty words. You'll need about forty words for a twenty-second PSA, therefore, sixty words for a thirty-second PSA, and so on. Of course, you will have to add time for any pauses. The stiffer the competition for air time, the more likely you will be to place the shorter, ten-second PSA.

Always type your PSAs on bond paper, white or another neutral color. If you are sending more than one, type each PSA on a separate piece of paper. If you have letterhead stationery, use it (if you don't, have some printed if you can afford to). Printed letterhead gives your announcement credibility by making it clear that you are not a fly-by-night group. Be sure to include in your letterhead that your group is nonprofit, if it is. If you cannot afford letterhead stationery, type your group's name and address at the top of the page, centered. Be neat; don't send out a PSA with typographical errors. Name a contact person, and include a phone number and a date for release. The words PUBLIC SERVICE ANNOUNCEMENT should appear in

NEWS

AMERICAN CANCER SOCIETY
Massachusetts Division
247 Commonwealth Avenue
Boston, MA 02116
1-800-952-7664
(617) 267-2650

PUBLIC SERVICE ANNOUNCEMENT   FOR USE BEGINNING SEPTEMBER 28
ROAD TO RECOVERY
10 SECONDS

ANNCR: Many cancer patients need transportation to

                      and from treatments. If you can spare a few

                      hours a month, you can drive somebody along

                      the road to recovery. Call your American Cancer

                      Society for details.

                                   #

AMERICAN
CANCER
SOCIETY®

Sample PSA. (Courtesy American Cancer Society.)

bold letters beneath the letterhead. The number of seconds required to read the PSA, and a word count, should also be included.

In writing your announcement, always be concise. Messages transmitted by radio leave little time for reflection. Your announcement is best kept quick and simple, therefore, but it must also be complete. Always include the who, what, where, when, and why. Although your PSA will ultimately comprise few words, they must be precise and well chosen. In a longer PSA you can elaborate slightly, but don't be surprised or offended if the radio station whittles your sixty-second announcement down to thirty.

PSAs should be written in "broadcast style"—that is, directly and simply. Because your words will be spoken by an announcer, not read by the audience, your tone should be conversational. Avoid complex sentence structures; each sentence should express a single thought. Use the active voice whenever possible (for example, write, "The car struck the boy" instead of "The boy was struck by the car"). Avoid editorializing; state the facts the way a reporter would. The broadcasting style makes far more use of indirect quotes than direct quotes, so paraphrase whenever appropriate. Avoid using acronyms; you would write *Merrymakers Acting Guild*, for example, instead of *MAG*. After preparing the PSA have several individuals read it aloud "cold" to see if they can understand it and read it smoothly, without making mistakes. If they tend to mispronounce words or stumble over awkward phrases, you should rework the copy. Smooth it out; remove the rough language.

Here are a few examples of effective PSAs:

Ten-Second PSA
Watch out for a driver who drives in spurts . . . ignores traffic signals . . . drives without headlights. This person is a drinking driver. Stay clear! Consider reporting him. The Prevention Center, North Shore Council on Alcoholism.

North Shore Council on Alcoholism
Danvers, Massachusetts

Twenty-Second PSA
It's a crime to waste water. . . . Don't be criminal. Here's a helpful tip on conserving water. Check all faucets in your home for leaks. Remember, even a tiny leak could waste up to fifteen gallons a day. This has been a message from the Department of Environmental Quality Engineering.

Massachusetts Department
of Environmental Quality Engineering

Thirty-Second PSA
MOVE FOR EQUALITY—Join the Boston chapter of the

National Organization for Women on August 28 for a "PAC-Woman Move-a-thon." Bike, jog, skate, or walk ten miles to benefit NOW's Political Action Committees. The route begins and ends at Boston Common with registration at 9:00 A.M., a kickoff rally at 10:00, and speakers and entertainment in the afternoon. For more information, call Boston NOW at 661-6015. That's 661-6015.

Boston NOW*

Public Affairs Programs

Cultivating radio contacts can pay off with an invitation to participate in a public affairs program. Of course, you don't have to wait to be invited; you can always ask to participate. Familiarize yourself with any public affairs programs that your local radio stations offer, and monitor them regularly. Express interest in participating by writing or phoning the public affairs director. Outline what you want to talk about, what audience you think will be interested, and how you feel your topic reflects viable community issues. Point out the controversy surrounding the topic and suggest ways that a program can be set up to include several persons. Being familiar with the station's programs, you will already know their formats—talk show, citizen editorial, phone-in program, meet the press—and their audiences. You will thus be able to plan your performance by tailoring your topic to fit the program's format and purpose. As with the newspaper interview, there are no set standards for making an effective and entertaining showing on a radio program, only general rules to follow.

Be sure your spokesperson, if other than yourself, is thoroughly knowledgeable about your organization, its purpose and overall goals. Spokespeople should always be ready with specifics, such as the date the group was founded, type of membership, officers (if any), facilities, and plans for the coming year. They should be lively, articulate, and capable of holding the audience's interest; they should be able to tell your story accurately and believably, in terms that the audi-

* PSAs reprinted with permission.

ence can readily grasp. They should be friendly, personable, and able to bring out the important issues in a sincere way, with appeal and salesmanship. They should contemplate, before going on the show, just what they would like to say, what is the most important point to make, how they can best get the basic facts across, what questions they will be asked, and how best they can answer them.

It may be helpful to prep your spokesperson by acting as the radio station host and posing questions. Write on index cards every question that is likely to be asked, then formulate answers to these questions as succinctly as possible. Practice delivery; refine any answers that sound stilted, evasive, or inadequate. Your spokesperson should not memorize the answers or avoid elaborating on them. Keep in mind, though, that radio does not lend itself well to complex explanations; in an attempt to keep the program moving, the announcer may not allow sufficient time to reflect or elaborate. Spokespeople should speak crisply and convincingly, and they should never assume that listeners start out interested in what they have to say or knowledgeable about their subject.

Radio announcers are as concerned about sound as they are about content. Spokespeople should have clear and authoritative voices; they should at all times project through sound a familiar and assuring image. Raspy, whiny, or stuttering voices should not be employed, nor should voices with foreign accents, if you can avoid it. Spokespeople should practice enunciating slowly and clearly without sounding rehearsed, monotonous, or snooty. At all times they should try to imagine what they sound like to the average listener.

If you are involved in a panel discussion, be sure to participate fully, but don't monopolize the conversation. Neutralize potential disagreements by remaining friendly and personable at all times. Use the other participants' first names, as well as the host's. Stay alert even if the conversation sways away from your area of interest; show hosts have a way of suddenly changing subjects, and you wouldn't want to be caught off guard. Above all, refrain from getting angry or sounding shrill on a program, no matter how threatened you feel. Anger turns people off, especially listeners, whom you are trying to persuade. If you remain cool under fire and calm under stress, you will project a reassuring, self-confident image, which will reflect positively on your organization and cause.

The same holds true for phone-in shows, when you are the guest whom listeners can phone to ask questions on the air. Sometimes you will get off-the-wall or utterly hostile questions. Once again, it is important to remain calm and friendly and answer as directly as possible. Make as much sense out of the question as you can. If the question is impertinent or ridiculous, or if the questioner totally misunderstands the issue, don't hesitate to say something like "That's really a misconception," and explain why. Or say, "That doesn't directly relate to my group's activities, but it reminds me of a more pertinent issue," and then elaborate. Use the opportunity to make an important statement that you might not have fit in otherwise. Address listeners by their first names to create a sense of authority and familiarity. Don't be afraid to ask a caller to clarify a question; in this way you may be able to disarm a potentially hostile questioner and take control of the situation.

The Citizen Editorial on Radio

If you are invited to give a citizen editorial on the radio, again strive to maintain a clear and friendly tone and follow the general principles discussed for public affairs programs. Editorials can be tricky; it is too easy to be preachy. Refrain from sounding aggravated; avoid any personal attack, or what could be construed as a personal attack, on groups or individuals opposed to your point of view. The FCC specifically prohibits attacks on "honesty, character, integrity, or like personal qualities," and radio stations usually screen editorials with this in mind. If you approach the editorial, which may run only fifty seconds, with persuasion instead of argumentation in mind, you will usually fare well. It is important to remember that radio stations are bound by rules of fairness and are thereby obligated to air all relevant viewpoints on controversial issues. The radio station that asks you for a citizen editorial, therefore, may be planning to have your adversaries present a rebuttal.

The following commentary was presented on radio station WCRB in Boston.

Citizen Editorial

"Ill fares the land, to hastening ills a prey, / Where wealth accumulates, and men decay." In the year 1770 Oliver Goldsmith wrote these stanzas about his native England. Do they apply to contemporary America?

President Reagan has some difficult choices to make. Projected deficits in the federal budget for 1982 have been estimated at $100 billion. This is about double the deficit for the last year of the Carter administration. For 1983 and 1984, present trends indicate deficits of at least $150 billion and $250 billion. These deficits are the result of a slowdown in business activity and the large cuts in personal and corporate taxes.

The president would seem to have to choose between five possible courses of action. First, he may choose to accept the deficits, thus rejecting fifty years of Republican rhetoric about the necessity—indeed, the sanctity—of a balanced federal budget. In fact, administration spokesmen have already begun to soft-pedal the importance of balancing the budget.

Second, President Reagan could yield to the considerable body of opinion that favors cuts in military spending. This would also violate conservative doctrine and would seem to undercut the Reagan response to the perceived Soviet threat —that we arm to parley. Further, it would diminish U.S. pressures upon Japan and Western Europe to increase *their* expenditures for armaments.

Third, he could try to reduce entitlement programs such as Social Security and Medicare. This would be very difficult in a recession and in an election year. Fourth, he might cut state and local grants even more than he has already, thus incurring the wrath of Republicans in power at those levels. Fifth, the President could attempt to raise taxes, which he is adamantly opposed to doing and which would be contrary to the mood of the voters.

Early indications are that the administration will seek

increases in taxes on consumption. Trial balloons have focused on tax increases on alcohol, tobacco, and gasoline, but are likely to spread to other consumer goods. Such tax increases would not violate Reaganomics' supply-side theory and would extend the new tax policy that shifts the burden from upper-income to lower-income people. It would also be in line with the favoritism toward the wealthy that this administration has already shown and that continues the trend begun under previous administrations, including that of Carter the Democrat. The Trickle-Down Theory seems to be enshrined in the United States, and the average taxpayer will continue to bear an unfair burden of our common needs. For we are rapidly becoming a society in which "wealth accumulates and men decay."

> *Jerome Grossman*
> *Executive Director*
> *Council for a Liveable World*
> *January 11, 1982**

Regardless whether you agree or disagree with Grossman's editorial remarks, you can learn from them. The editorial is ultimately persuasive because it is clear and logical. Even though editorials are supposed to feature one's opinions, the writer's judgments are initially restrained. By using the quote from an eighteenth-century poet, Oliver Goldsmith, he creates an impression of objectivity. The quote does several things: it introduces the theme; it objectifies the editorial; and it adds punch to the opening because the language is archaic and rhymed—two characteristics that help to snare the listener's attention.

Mr. Grossman goes on to say that Goldsmith's words are relevant to contemporary America. The historical comparison adds weight to Grossman's ideas. He then states simply that President Reagan has difficult choices to make concerning the federal deficit, and he describes these choices in five points:

POINT 1:   Deficit can be accepted;

POINT 2:   Cuts in military spending can be made;

POINT 3:   Entitlement programs can be reduced;

* Reprinted with permission.

POINT 4 :   State and local grants can be cut; and

POINT 5 :   Taxes can be raised.

The points are clearly enumerated, and keyed by the words *first, second,* and so on. Not until the last paragraph do we find an explicit statement of Mr. Grossman's opinion, and the point of his editorial—"that the average taxpayer will continue to bear an unfair burden. . . ." If he stated that at the outset, it would make far less of an impact. Instead, he first makes the audience receptive to him; then he makes a point-by-point analysis, from which his conclusion logically follows.

Grossman ties the editorial together nicely by repeating part of Goldsmith's quote at the conclusion. His last sentence reminds us of the beginning, reasserts the relevance of Goldsmith's quote, and affirms Grossman's viewpoint on President Reagan's economic policies. Goldsmith seems to speak for Grossman in the last phrase, which echoes and settles in our ears with the weight of two hundred years.

This editorial formula is successful for Grossman, but you should not restrict yourself to following it. Trying to mimic someone else's style can be disastrous; few things expose insincerity faster than affected language. Nonetheless, I have analyzed the structure and effect of this editorial to stress the importance of finesse. Delivering an editorial can be tricky, with as much to lose as there is to gain. It is fine to express strong opinions, but in order to be persuasive you must build your arguments solidly, speak in subdued tones, and make your statements credible. One more note: this particular editorial was well placed on radio, but it would have been too stirring for television. Because television is a visual as well as an auditory medium, televised messages are inherently more intense than radio messages. A strong statement, when televised, can easily offend the audience. Grossman's editorial would have been less effective on television; it would have sounded somewhat inflammatory and could have discredited the speaker.

If you disagree with an editorial presented by a station's management, the station will usually let you make a rebuttal on the air, as a New Hampshire citizen has done in the following example.

Station Editorial

Last week New Hampshire citizens held their annual town meetings. One question asked: Should the New Hampshire congressional delegation support a U.S. resolution requesting the president to propose to the Soviet Union that the United States and Russia adopt a mutual freeze on the testing, production, and deployment of nuclear weapons?

It was not enough to consider gutters and curbing, storm windows for schools, and licensing of dogs. Now New Hampshire citizens had to consider an international and frightening issue—the nuclear arms race.

The issue had come to the town meetings by default. Yes, because our national government has not been able to address effectively and realistically this most crucial question. In our opinion, the people of New Hampshire—and the United States—have been let down by our military strategists, our biggest corporations, and our Washington legislators. The military strategists have told us that we need more nuclear weapons in order to be more secure, but we know that more weapons will only make us less secure because the Russians must then respond by matching our expanding arsenal. Large corporations have told us that military production is good for the economy, but we believe that huge military production generates less wealth and less long-term employment than nonmilitary production.

Many Washington legislators have told us that Reagan's total budget, including its monstrous nuclear weapons provisions, must be approved in order to insure economic recovery. But we think that many legislators support this insane budget only because they fear disagreeing with a popular president.

And while we are most encouraged by the proposal, introduced last week in Congress, calling for a mutual nuclear weapons freeze between the United States and Russia, we must remind ourselves that our legislators took action only after they had received an overwhelming mandate from their constituency. The nuclear weapons freeze has received such sweeping citizen support that it will probably be on the ballot in California, Michigan, Delaware, and New Jersey. In Massachusetts alone, a form of the proposal passed the House and Senate last summer, and over seventy-five thousand people in Massachusetts have signed the freeze petition.

If you would like to join these people, and the forty-eight towns of New Hampshire that passed the freeze proposal, a very exciting opportunity is open to you. Join other Americans on June 12 when they rally at the United Nations in New York City to support the special U.N. session on nuclear disarmament. Your presence June 12, along with hundreds of thousands of others, may be the message needed to impress Washington and Moscow that the ordinary citizen will no longer tolerate what we feel is irresponsibility on this issue. This rally may well be one of the most important town meetings of this century. Will you be there?

Ted Jones
President, WCRB
Boston, Massachusetts
March 18, 1982

Citizen's Rebuttal

My name is Norman Geis and I am a resident of Kensington, New Hampshire. I am responding to a recent WCRB editorial by station president Ted Jones concerning our town meetings and nuclear weapons freeze articles. You may remember the editorial—it used phrases like "frightening issue," "monstrous nuclear weapons," "insane budget," "overwhelming mandate," and, finally, "sweeping citizen support."

It's time to look at a few facts to see how shallow the freeze support really is. We have 653 registered voters in Kensington, and about 175 were in the hall for the town meeting. This attendance ratio is typical of many New Hampshire and New England towns.

I offered the following alternative to the typical freeze article in our warrant: "Resolved: It is the sense of the Kensington Town Meeting of 1982 that we support the efforts of the administration and the Congress to reduce, and eventually eliminate, the nuclear weapons of the United States, the Soviet Union, and other countries while remaining committed to our national objective of peace through strength."

This alternative amendment was defeated by a hand count of sixty-three to fifty-three. The six-vote difference represented only 1% of those registered and less than 3% of

those present in the hall. The freeze article then passed by
voice vote. These facts just cannot justify the media claims
for overwhelming support sweeping the country. Well-organized special interest groups have exploited these town meetings to create the illusion of a "grass-roots" movement.

I believe politicians and editors should stop using inflammatory adjectives to play upon people's fears, and start
a reasoned analysis of what will truly stimulate the Soviets
to seriously negotiate nuclear weapon reductions. History
tells us by repeated example that an inferior military pos-
ture, a divided population, and a temporizing appeasement
will not do it.

I'm just one New Hampshire citizen, but that's the way
it looks to me.

Norman Geis
April 22, 1982*

The Impromptu Interview

Having developed radio contacts and invited them to cover
your meetings and special events, you will inevitably be
asked for an impromptu interview. Such interviews are a
basic part of a publicist's job, but they can also be intimi-
dating if you are caught unprepared. Your objective is clear
and simple: relate a bit of accurate and timely information
about your group or the importance of the activity in progress. Before such an activity begins, consider the most important point to make, and arrive with a theme in mind.
The radio reporter, who may look like a high school student,
will stick a microphone in your face and ask, "What is the
purpose of this meeting?" Your comments will be taped on
a cassette tape recorder. Experience will teach you that you
should answer quickly and succinctly. Most often your response will be edited and aired on the radio in a different
context, so that the announcer's question seems to lead directly into one of your remarks. Short, simple sentences are
safest, since they don't rely on qualifying statements that
may be omitted in the broadcast. Such impromptu interviews are often carried out over the phone; your responses,

* Station editorial and citizen's rebuttal reprinted with permission.

again, are recorded. If you keep in mind what the radio reporter wants to know, stick to a few prepared comments, and remain focused, you will usually fare pretty well. After all, as your group's media coordinator, you are an authority on its activities and goals. Use that authority to your advantage.

6.

The Wizardry of Television

TELEVISION, being bound by the same broadcasting laws as radio, offers similar opportunities for free publicity to nonprofit organizations. Although the rules are the same, the methods for winning free broadcast time are somewhat different. Most organizations are eager to place publicity—in the form of a news spot, calendar listing, PSA, or public affairs spot—on local television, and rightfully so. The power of television is self-evident; its ability to persuade an audience is unparalleled by any other medium, and it has come to dominate the communications world. Even when they report only local news, television news staffs are large, often consisting of several hundred people. The equipment at a typical station is complex and expensive; as a result, a sixty-second advertisement on a local station can cost thousands of dollars, depending on the size of the audience. Television is capable of focusing the attention of an entire community on a single issue—heady stuff for the practical publicist. How do you go about enlisting the help of such a powerful medium?

The first step to take is a familiar one. Systematically identify and list all the television stations serving your area, and make a chart similar to the one for radio stations. Identify the station, its address and phone number, and contacts such as the news director, station director, public affairs director, and reporters, all of whose names you can obtain simply by calling the station. Find out whether or not the station is affiliated with a network (CBS, NBC, or ABC), independently owned and operated, publicly owned, or cable (supported by subscriptions). This will help you determine how much time the station devotes to locally oriented broadcasts. Most stations have a local news show, and many have public affairs programs (such as a citizens' round table, face-the-state program, or interview session), community calendars, and editorials presented by citizens. Include the names of these shows and the times they are broadcast on your chart as well. Find out whether your local stations have written policies regarding their public services; many television stations do. If possible, obtain copies of such policies; they will be very helpful in locating publicity opportunities. When in doubt, phoning or writing the public affairs director is the most direct way to get information on a station's public affairs policies.

Many stations provide help to nonprofit groups in preparing informational spots and PSAs. Work directly with public affairs directors when you can, but remember that most are very busy, and be careful not to take up too much of their time. Remember, many other groups are competing for free air time.

Because there are far fewer television stations than radio stations in any area, it is easy to identify those that serve your community simply by using the yellow pages of your phone book. Los Angeles is the nation's second largest television market—that is, the potential audience for its stations is the second largest in the country. With between four and five million households that own TVs, Los Angeles has only sixteen television stations. Madison, Wisconsin, is the nation's 102nd largest television market, with about two hundred thousand households that own TVs. In Madison there are only four stations. It is a relatively simple matter to call or write these stations, whether in Los Angeles or Madison, to find out what public services they provide. Most will readily supply you with a list of contacts and locally produced programs.

Identifying Television Contacts

A typical TV station in a moderate-sized city may have one to two hundred employees. As a publicist, you are interested in the news and public affairs divisions. The public affairs director and the public service director are the first people to contact. They can usually tell you all you need to know about the station's public affairs programs and other services, and they should be included on all media lists. In the news department you should be able to identify several more key contacts. They will include the news director, who oversees the news staff and broadcasts; the assignment editor, who ensures that the major stories and beats are covered and assigns reporters to stories; the news producer, who determines what reports will be aired; and the reporters, who may cover stories relevant to your cause and who are often under pressure to come up with story ideas.

In order to ensure that your news release, newsletter, or personal letter is received by the right person, each of the titles listed here should be included on your chart. It is usually best, however, to work directly with reporters interested in your topic. Telephone them immediately after sending a news release or other information. Because TV reporters have considerable freedom to pursue stories, they can help determine whether your activities are covered in the news.

TV news and public affairs programs vary depending on the station's location and affiliation. Nonetheless, you can get an idea of the variety and number of these services by examining the program schedule of any local station. WBZ-

Station	Channel/Affiliate	PSAs	Public Affairs Programs	News	Contacts
WKBC One Waston Pl. Atlanta, GA 223-2500	9/CBS	10, 30 secs.	Citizen editorials Community Affairs Round Table Evening Magazine	12:00 P.M. 6:00 P.M. 11:00 P.M.	Jack Spann, news Ellen Moore, public affairs Gwynne Jones, Round Table Chuck Aikens, Evening Magazine
WLMX 116 Arrow Rd. Atlanta, GA 666-9916	11/ABC	10, 20, 30, 60 secs.	Community calendar Speak Out	10:00 A.M. 6:00 P.M. 11:00 P.M.	Herman Runyan, news Steven Miller, public affairs Bill Herbert, community calendar Ralph Pepper, Speak Out
WLIS 12 Checks Ave. Decatur, GA 226-7919	2/NBC	10, 30 secs.	Community calendar Meet the Press Update Community Focus	8:00 A.M. 6:00 P.M. 11:00 P.M.	Marjorie Loughton, news Louise Johnson, public affairs Dwayne Williams, Meet the Press Mary Framm, Update Lori Mockingbird, Community Focus
WDMZ 90 Franklin Ave. Savannah, GA 442-5142	22/Independent	none	Speak Out Make-a-Date Georgia Globe	10:00 P.M.	Ralph Noone, news Kim Carrin, public affairs Ron Smith, Speak Out
WEDA 3100 Silver Pl. Atlanta, GA 662-3888	40/Independent	10, 20, 30, 40, 50, 60 secs.	Citizen editorials Community calendar Bells-Are-Ringing	12:00 P.M. 5:00 P.M.	David Jones, news Carol Notte, public affairs Beth Stevens, Bells-Are-Ringing

Sample television chart. All information presented here has been invented.

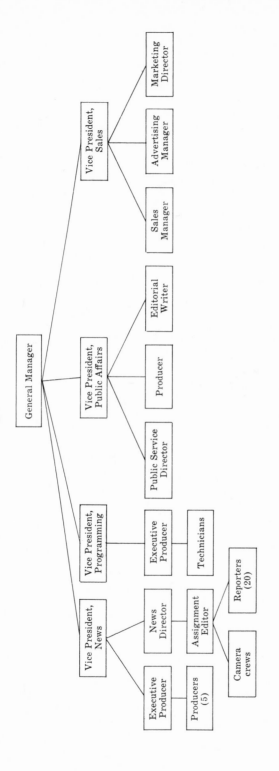

The generalized organization of a television station. Most stations have large staffs, sometimes reaching into the hundreds. Key contacts should include the vice president for news, the news director, the assignment editor, and individual reporters, as well as the vice president for public affairs and members of the public affairs staff, such as the public service director and the editorial writer.

TV in Boston, for example, lists the following programs provided to its Boston market, which is the sixth largest in the country:

Newsroom Hotline. A special phone line that allows people to call the station's reporters directly to tip them off on fast-breaking stories.

Eyewitness News Almanac. An early morning news show that broadcasts local and national news. Specific contact.

First 4 News. An early evening news show that airs just prior to the evening news show. Specific contact.

Eyewitness News. The station's full-scale evening news show, which airs at 6:00 P.M. and 11:00 P.M. Specific contact.

The I-Team. A special group of investigative reporters who cover a broad scope of social, economic, and political topics for the "Eyewitness News" show.

I-Team Hotline. A special phone line that allows people to tip off the investigative team.

Impact Series. A monthly program that explores a local issue through reports, studio interviews, or citizens' comments. Specific contact.

Woman. A weekday program with a live magazine format and studio audience. It focuses on the interests of contemporary women. Specific contact.

Evening Magazine. A weekday program with a magazine format. Topics of general interest are explored. The topics range nationwide, but many focus on Boston. Specific contact.

Moneysense. A locally produced program that offers tips for consumers and budget planners. Specific contact.

Coming Together. A weekly program that examines topics of interest to blacks and urban residents. Interviews and features. Specific contact.

Eyewitness News Conference. A Sunday program that features panelists who direct questions to a local news maker or discuss a local issue. Specific contact.

For Kids Only. A weekly program featuring local junior high school students, who interview celebrities and news makers of their choice. Specific contact.

Nosotros. A weekly program concerning subjects of interest to the Spanish-speaking community. Some films shown are in Spanish. Specific contact.

Community Auditions. A weekly program featuring local amateur talent. Specific contact.

A Show of Faith. Discusses the influence of religion on individuals and organizations in today's society. Explores the nature of faith. Specific contact.

Prime Time. A weekly program that features subjects of interest to the elderly population. Specific contact.

Speak Out. Allows viewers to comment on camera on subjects of personal and community concern. Fifty-second messages, 135 words in length, are aired four times.

Soap Box. Same feature as the above, only this program is for people under sixteen years old.

Public Service Announcements. Nonprofit groups can place PSAs through the public affairs director. Professional assistance is provided.

Community News Notes. Nonprofit groups can publicize events over the air by sending messages to the public affairs director.

For whichever program you wish to participate in or service you wish to use, there is a specific person to contact, address to write to, or phone number to call. You need not try to use all the programs on your local station; by intelligently selecting news shows and public services and targeting your publicity accordingly you will have the best chance of winning air time. Other television stations may have programs and services different from those described here. You'll need to identify the most attractive publicity outlets for each station in your area. Once again, a few well-placed and well-timed inquiries are far more effective than a slew of press releases and letters sent at random.

The Television PSA

A PSA is perhaps the best tool for inexpensively getting your message across on local television. Television PSAs are prepared like radio PSAs; they are typically presented in time spots ranging from ten to sixty seconds. Most stations prefer the thirty-second spot, although twenty-second and sixty-second spots are also popular. Your copy should be brief and succinct, typed double-spaced on an 8½-by-11-inch sheet of paper. Be sure to include your group's name at the top, a statement that the group is nonprofit (if it is), the name and phone number of a contact person, a word count, the time spot needed (use the rule for radio PSAs: ten seconds for every twenty words), and the length of time the announcement is usable (three months, for example). Remember that your words will be spoken; avoid difficult phrases and complex sentences.

A television PSA should be accompanied by one or more slides, which will make up the video portion of your announcement. Each slide should be 35 millimeters, in color and glass-mounted (cardboard-mounted slides tend to warp and thus result in unclear images). If your PSA is only ten seconds long, you probably will be unable to use more than two slides; usually one is sufficient. For longer PSAs you may want to include a series of slides. You have the option of using pictorial slides, word slides, or a combination of the two. For instance, if you are submitting a 20-second PSA on your community's drug rehabilitation center, you might want to include a slide of the center's interior or exterior. You would also want to include a phone number, which can be superimposed on the first slide or included on a separate word slide, called a *tag*. Be sure to allow sufficient time for your tag to appear with your phone

Voice-over: Looking to adopt a child? Call the Massachusetts Adoption Resource Exchange at 451-1460. A child is waiting.

Ten-second PSA. (Courtesy Massachusetts Adoption Resource Exchange.)

number, and perhaps have the announcer, or *voice-over*, read the number aloud. Station managers do not like to have their switchboards deluged with calls from people who could not write down your number in time.

Be sure your slides are properly exposed and in sharp focus. Don't try to be fancy, just illustrate your copy clearly and realistically. If you need help preparing your slides, ask the station's public affairs director. Stations provide this service to nonprofit groups; however, the less time your PSA demands of the station's staff, the more likely it will be aired. If you want to include music, prepare a standard PSA with slides and ask the public affairs director if music could be arranged by the station.

Word slides can be inexpensively made by lettering a board with transfer type and having a professional photographer make a slide from it. If you have a choice, specify colors for the type and the background. Usually a dark background (black or blue) and bright lettering (yellow or green) works best on a word slide. A professional photographer can also superimpose words on a pictorial slide inexpensively; just provide a lettered board along with your color slide. Depending on the background, superimposed words are printed in black or *reversed out* so they appear in white; make sure your telephone number won't be hard to read because it is too close in color to your picture.

The criteria television stations use to select PSAs vary, but you can expect them to follow a few general guidelines. First, they will favor nonprofit organizations that are reputable, trustworthy, and readily identified. Fly-by-night groups stand little chance of clearing the public service director's desk. Commercial organizations place PSAs on occasion, but rarely are they allowed to identify themselves even by placing their logo on the tag. (Nonprofit groups, too, should refrain from highlighting their names; the purpose of a PSA is to inform, not to promote a particular organization.) Groups submitting PSAs must also be locally based; few stations are interested in giving valuable broadcast time for a cause irrelevant to its viewers. Most PSAs that are aired fall into one of three categories: those concerning social problems, such as crime; those concerning health and safety services, such as flu shots or free clinics; and those concerning educational and training opportunities, such as adult education at the local high school. Other topics are given time, but usually these are preferred.

Consider your target stations before sending a PSA. If a station does not have a strong commitment to broadcast-

Voice-over: 319 young adults in Massachusetts thought they'd be alive to see this commercial. But they died last year in drunk driving accidents. Their chances of having an accident were 25 times greater because of drinking. So, instead of seeing this commercial, they're in it.

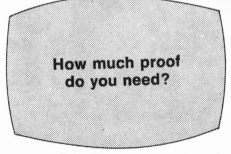

Voice-over: How much proof do you need?

Thirty-second PSA. Ten slides of young adults are flashed consecutively. The voice-over begins after the third slide is shown. (Courtesy Massachusetts Governor's Highway Safety Bureau and Kenyon and Eckhardt, Inc.)

ing such announcements, you are better off concentrating on other outlets. The strength of the station's financial base frequently determines the amount of air time it can give away; as a rule, stations that sell more advertising (and therefore make more money) are apt to run more PSAs. You should also consider each station's schedule. More PSAs are shown in the winter and summer than in the spring and fall. This is because new shows usually begin in the spring and fall; hence, the numbers of viewers are at their peak in these seasons, and competition for air time is particularly stiff. Be sure to time your submission so that it coincides with a station's season. Although three-month viewing periods for PSAs are preferred, if you send a PSA with a three-month life span in late summer, the station may air it for a much shorter period of time before revising its entire schedule for the fall.

Finally, whenever you send a PSA you should include several copies (keep one, too, of course) and a newsletter or fact sheet giving background information on your organization. Clearly label all parts of the package (including the package itself) with your organization's name, contact person, phone number, and address, and the PSA's word count, duration, life span, and title (a few words identifying your group or the subject of your announcement). This will make the public affairs director's job much easier.

The Television Interview

Television interviews can be disturbing, especially impromptu ones. As your group's spokesperson, you are most likely to be interviewed on the spot at a rally, a public meeting, or another major event. The television crew, which consists of an on-camera reporter, a cameraperson, and often a sound person, will have been sent by the assignment editor of your local station, and any report they make will probably be aired on the next news show. Lasting anywhere from one to five minutes, their report is likely to include interviews with several persons, each of whom will answer one or two short questions. The practical publicist should always anticipate when and where the television crew may turn up, what types of questions they may ask, and what should be said to the audience in a very short time span. This last is especially important, because television does not lend itself to complex issues and answers. How much can you explain in thirty seconds?

Although television has a powerful impact on a community at large, it also has a tendency to reduce complex issues to mere slogans. It is often more important to consider what you *shouldn't* say, therefore, than what you *should* say. To the practical publicist, the challenge of television is to make a pertinent statement concerning a serious issue in a very short time while projecting a positive and persuasive image. This can be difficult to do, especially when a camera is zeroing in on you, hot lights are flashing in your eyes, and a reporter is firing questions while distracting you with a microphone. Here are a few simple, television-wise suggestions that may help.

Some publicists like to forget that the camera, the lights, and the microphone are there; they try to ignore the whole assembly of electronic equipment. Whether you can do so or not, you should focus your attention on the reporters, and speak to them as if they were newspaper reporters. Television is a personal medium; it demands a conversational tone and speech. Use simple words and sentences, and be as direct as possible. Don't look for the camera; instead, keep a natural pose and let the camera find you. Try not to show hostility or anger if a question disturbs you; remain friendly and calm. Refrain from talking too fast; stand up straight, and speak distinctly and clearly. If you are asked a question that you do not know how to answer, be honest and say so. It is better to say you don't know than to fake it and end up babbling or saying something incorrect. When pressed by reporters, simply reiterate that you don't know the answer, but that you will contact them when you have it. Remember, you have no control over the editing of the video tape; you may be denied the opportunity to compensate for your errors.

Your appearance is also important on television. Besides communicating verbally, you are communicating visually. A neat and well-groomed spokesperson, therefore, is most effective and credible. Dress conservatively; avoid loud plaids, elaborate prints, entirely dark or stark white outfits, shiny jewelry, and any other distracting apparel. Dress to suit the occasion; if you represent a commercial fishermen's association, for example, and a television crew wants to interview you on a trawler or at a wharf, don't dress in a three-piece business suit. If you are asked to come to the television studio, conversely, don't show up in a slicker or oilskin. Hairstyles should also be conservative. Spokeswomen in particular should remember this; elaborate coiffures distract the viewer and may appear somewhat comic when the camera zooms in. To make a good impression on your audience, you should look credible, neat, honest, and intelligent. Because the viewer has only a few seconds to form an opinion of you, that opinion will be based largely on your appearance.

For longer interviews you should follow these same guidelines; however, you will have more opportunity to get your message across. Because arrangements will be made in advance, you will have time to prepare yourself. Use this time wisely: determine where you want the interview to take place and what you would like to say. A room such as an office, conference room, or library usually offers the most privacy and adequate space. Check on the availability of electric outlets, because the lights used by the crew require more watts that the typical outlet can provide. They may need to use several outlets on different circuits so that they don't blow a fuse.

Select a room that is clean, uncluttered and, if possible, warmly decorated. The camera will inevitably focus on your surroundings, which are a direct reflection on you and your organization. If the weather permits, you might hold the interview outdoors. An outdoor interview has a softer, more restful quality, especially if it is held in a garden or park on a warm, sunny day. Such a setting can help if your interviewer has a reputation for being hostile. An outdoor interview has another advantage: it can reinforce your theme.

If you are concerned about housing rehabilitation in your neighborhood, for example, you might arrange to hold the interview before a house that is being renovated. Or, if you are concerned about water pollution, you might hold the interview before a polluted body of water, perhaps where the discharge of pollutants can be seen. Your interview thus becomes a kind of show and tell.

Try to anticipate the reporter's questions, then prepare brief and simple answers. You may want to write down several statements you would like to make on the air. A bit of play-acting can help you refine your delivery as well as your answers. Have an associate pose as the reporter, and practice delivering your answers—not word-for-word, but in an easy, conversational style and tone. Practice before a mirror (or with a video recorder, if you have access to one) so that you can see what you look like when speaking. Note mannerisms such as ear-pulling, nose-scratching, slouching, or covering your face with your hands, and get rid of these mannerisms. You may never get to deliver your prepared responses (unless you are particularly good at anticipating questions), but the practice will help when you must answer questions on camera. By simply paying close attention to interviews on your television set, you can see what works effectively and what does not. You will find that the effective communicator speaks clearly and to the point, and is personable. Try to relax during your interview. Take your time answering questions, and be forthright, honest, and confident.

The Citizen Editorial on Television

The same general rules apply to television editorials. If you are invited to make an editorial broadcast, however, you will have several advantages. First, you will be able to use a script (which often has to be submitted in advance), and you will have more time to rehearse. You will be free to choose a topic and to direct your attack as you see fit. You will also have more air time in which to explain complex issues, and you won't have to worry about being sidetracked by a reporter's questioning. So make good use of these advantages: strike a balance between objective and persuasive statements, and explain issues sufficiently. Avoid such phrases as "I believe . . ." and "We feel . . . ," which make you sound hesitant and highlight the fact that you are expressing only an opinion. Don't be afraid to give your point of view, but give it calmly and graciously, not with a bible-thumping drive. Remember that you are not a preacher, and that most people do not like to be preached at. The TV editorial that follows will give you an idea of what stations allow.

Citizen Editorial

Recently psychiatry has been branded a bogus science—one that can't have experts because it lacks expertise. Nothing could be further from the truth. Psychiatry is as reliable as almost any branch of medicine. Psychiatry has been scapegoated because of insanity pleas. Long before psychiatrists, there was an insanity defense. Insanity is a legal, not medical, term. A psychiatrist doesn't rule someone sane. A court does that. Psychiatry merely presents medical testimony. Our legal system is grounded in adversity. One party argues a proposition; the other denies it. There's no room for blending expert opinion in cross-examination. Psychiatrists have no desire to condone crime or be jailers in white coats. Society, not psychiatry, decides whether someone is guilty or insane.

John P. Callan, M.D.
Connecticut State Medical Society*

As with a radio editorial, you should speak simply, clearly, and personally. Always include the who, what, where, when, and why to ensure that your audience knows what your subject is. Avoid embellishments such as jokes or puns, but don't be afraid to use germane quotes, especially if they are from famous people. (One, however, is usually plenty.) Remember that speakers who pay respect to their adversaries before questioning the adversaries' views are usually better received. If you won't tone down a

* Reprinted with permission.

verbal attack for the sake of politeness, do so to comply with laws against slander and the fairness rule of the FCC, which ensures that an attack will always be met with a rebuttal. If you are the subject of an attack, take advantage of this rule by making a rebuttal—unless your opponent's argument is faulty or ridiculous, in which case your response would only add credence to it. Otherwise, calmly and systematically take apart your accuser's argument in your own editorial. Don't go for blood, go for embarrassment by pointing out ridiculous statements. Refrain from attacking the editorializer personally. Occasionally a vehement rebuttal works well, but they are tricky to pull off and are best avoided.

Following is a station editorial and a citizen's rebuttal to it.

Station Editorial

History was made in the state supreme court last week. For the first time, cameras were allowed to record court proceedings. We think this one-year experiment in openness is off to a good start. It's a program that's needed, for several reasons.

Most court sessions are open to the public, but few can attend. Court is held when most people are working, which makes even the most interesting and important case inaccessible to the majority of citizens. And over the years, a mystique has been built up around the courts. People think that judges are distant figures and that lawyers talk in language the average person can't understand.

That's why more court reporting makes so much sense. It makes at least some cases accessible to nearly everyone. And it demystifies the courts.

This is only an experiment. There now are several rules that the media must follow before taking cameras into the courts. The goal of these rules—to give the courts some control over trial coverage—is understandable. But Channel 3 believes that Connecticut could learn from some other states —including Massachusetts and Rhode Island—that have not found it necessary to impose such restrictions.

The legal system deserves our respect. This respect comes from knowledge of the courts and the way they work.

And the best way to achieve that is through openness—the more the better.

WFSB
June 7, 1982*

Citizen's Rebuttal

Having convinced the Superior Court to allow cameras and other paraphernalia into Connecticut's courtrooms, Channel 3 now seeks to eliminate even the modest guidelines developed by the judiciary.

Channel 3 is involved in stiff competition in the newscast ratings game. Their gods are the Nielsen ratings and advertising revenue. They are not interested in justice or in educating the public. The news media will focus on the sensational and the grisly. It is unfair to force litigants in court to bear the burden of unrestricted television coverage.

The news media has a disturbing track record in covering judicial proceedings. Their insatiable appetite for sensationalism has turned every famous trial—from Lindberg to Dr. Sam Shepard to Klaus von Bulow—into a circus, a farce.

Too many persons have been denied a fair trial because of this. In such trials, the news media feeds us thirty-second, bang-bang, rock 'em–sock 'em clips of an entire day's trial testimony.

The function of our courts is to resolve disputes between persons and/or between the state and its citizens. With cameras, cameras everywhere, without control exercised by a disinterested judge, the quality of justice in Connecticut will nose-dive. How many rape victims want to describe their ordeal before thousands of viewers? And what about divorces, in which deeply personal aspects of the litigants' lives are exposed? Do we really have a right to view this? Hopefully, Channel 3 will reconsider its demand to turn the courts into a media show. If not, the people of Connecticut, and especially those persons responsible for the administration of justice, should reject Channel 3's attempt to destroy the dignity of the courtroom.

Attorney Paul N. Shapera of Hartford
June 16, 1982*

* Reprinted with permission.

7.

The Power of the Printed Word

PRINTED materials—pamphlets, newsletters, calling cards, posters, and letterhead stationery—are essential in any effective publicity campaign. Such publications represent one of the largest expenses of most nonprofit groups. If properly designed and printed, however, they usually prove to be worth far more than their production costs. They give your organization credibility by showing that it is not a fly-by-night group—that it is run professionally and effectively. They show that your cause is serious—that it merits printing.

The types of publications your group should produce depend on your finances, the audience you intend to reach, and your ultimate goals. Common types are described here, and inexpensive techniques and effective formats are suggested for each. You will need some basic art supplies, including a drawing board, T-square, ruler, nonphoto blue pencils, X-acto knife and spare blades, triangle, masking tape and cellophane tape, rubber cement, transfer type, and border tape. You will also need a fine-line black ink pen, such as a Pilot Razor Point, plain white paper for layouts, a reduction wheel, and nonphoto blue graph paper.

Letterhead Stationery

These stock items are relatively inexpensive to produce. For your letterhead stationery, use standard-sized (8½-by-11-inch) bond (writing-quality) paper, which comes in 16- to 24-pound weights. Design your letterhead simply with your organization's name, address, and phone number in the top two inches of the stationery. If yours is a nonprofit group, include mention of that; it will help you when you use your stationery to request free broadcast time and financial support. It will identify your group as one that is working not for money but for a cause. Occasionally groups include one line in their letterhead that describes what they do, or what their purpose is. Such a description is optional; if you include one, however, it should be brief and to the point.

Letterhead is usually typeset, by either a printing or a typesetting house, and printed by offset. Typesetters usually charge by the hour, but because the time required to set letterhead is minimal, so is the typesetting cost.

If you are unfamiliar with type sizes and faces, ask your typesetter for help. Contrary to popular belief, most typesetters are very willing to aid in the design of simple publications. If you write down exactly what you want to appear on your letterhead and point out which lines are most important, the typesetter will be able to determine appropriate type sizes. Type is measured in *points*. Although it is usually available in sizes ranging from 6- to 72-point, the biggest letters on your letterhead will probably not be more than 18- or 24-point.

The term *typeface* refers to the graphic design of the letters. There are literally hundreds of typefaces; your typesetter should have at least several available. Choose one that attracts you, but avoid getting very fancy; remember that

zpg-mass
14 Beacon Street, Room 707   Boston, MA 02108
Telephone (617) 742-6840

zpg-mass
14 Beacon St., Rm. 707
Boston, MA 02108

Letterhead stationery and matching envelope. (Courtesy Boston chapter of Zero Population Growth.)

your primary goal is to make your name known. If you have an example of a letterhead you like, your typesetter can probably match the type for you.

You must choose colors of both ink and paper for your letterhead stationery. The printer will be able to offer you papers in a selection of colors at the same price. Choose a light color—white, buff, ivory, cream, beige, or light gray. Stay away from green, blue, yellow, and other bright or dark colors. Choose ink of a dark color—either black, dark brown, or dark blue. If you want more than one color of ink it will cost you more, since you will incur extra setup charges. Of course, you will need to order blank sheets of bond paper in the same color as your letterhead stationery for letters that are longer than one page. You will also need to have business-size envelopes printed on the same paper with the same ink; your organization's name and address should appear in the upper left-hand corner.

Another important feature of most letterhead stationery is the logo. As a symbol of your organization or campaign, your logo will allow people to identify your group at a glance. We see logos every day, in the supermarket, the office, the high school, and the movie theater. They range from very simple designs, such as a triangle, to elaborate works of art. If you do not have access to a graphic artist who can design a logo for you, use a simple design. You may even just exaggerate your initials. Logos can be printed in several different sizes on one sheet of paper and used on everything you print for identification. Keep in mind that your logo should be original. Logos tend to retain their original identification with the public, and many are copyrighted.

To increase their credibility, some groups like to include the names of their officers or key members on their stationery, especially if these people are well-known members of the community. Campaigns that involve many different organizations usually list the participating groups on their letterhead.

Letterhead stationery comes in handy for billings, press releases, and PSAs. An easy way to turn your stationery into a press release form is to spell PRESS RELEASE with transfer type (at least 24-point) directly beneath your letterhead. Likewise, you can use your stationery for a PSA by labeling it PUBLIC SERVICE ANNOUNCEMENT. Because press releases and PSAs are usually sent to many contacts, you can letter a plain white piece of paper and have it photocopied onto your stationery.

zpg-mass
14 Beacon St., Rm. 707
Boston, MA 02108

71 capitol avenue hartford, conn. 06115

Logos. (Courtesy Connecticut Coastal Area Management Program, Boston chapter of Zero Population Growth, and the American Cancer Society.)

Calling Cards

These are recommended for any organization that seeks to enlist members or to develop media contacts. Calling cards are printed on card stock, about 65-pound weight. The typical calling card measures 3½ by 2 inches and simply displays the name of your organization, your logo, your address, your phone number, and your personal name. The calling card is great for introductions, especially at press conferences or large gatherings, where you will meet people who may wish to contact you later. They can be typeset inexpensively, but they should be printed in quantities of at least one thousand to take advantage of the bulk discount.

Newsletters

A newsletter is the voice of an organization. With circulations as high as several thousand, newsletters enable groups to address at length issues to which newspapers and magazines cannot devote such attention. A newsletter can cover a broad range of topics; it can serve as a public clearinghouse for books and articles on a group's concern; it can advertise upcoming meetings and events, special publications, and films; and it can inform a cross section of the population of your community.

Most newsletters are sent out quarterly—that is, once every three months. You probably won't want to publish more often, since even a bimonthly newsletter could keep you busy full time, and few groups can come up with enough worthy articles to fill a monthly publication. It is better to have too much to say than too little; you don't want your newsletter to be dull. What goes into your newsletter is a matter for your board of directors or editor to decide; it is your job to design a cost-effective format.

Several good formats are commonly used. The most favored is 8½ by 11 inches, with two columns per page and four to ten pages in length. A four-page newsletter this size is actually one sheet of paper, 11 by 17 inches, folded in half. On each page you should have two columns of copy, a

¾-inch margin on all sides, and a ½-inch *gutter*, or space between the columns. This means that the columns, or type blocks, will be 3¼ inches wide and 9½ inches long. Your first page will be shorter, of course; you will need at least three inches on the top for your heading, or *masthead*. The masthead is somewhat like a letterhead, only slightly more elaborate; it is the same in every edition you publish. It comprises the name of your newsletter in big letters, your logo, your address, and a line or two (in smaller letters) identifying the publication as, for example, "the newsletter of the Connecticut Coastal Management Program." With each issue you will add the date of publication, the volume number (volume one for the first year, volume two for the second year, and so on), and the issue number. It may be worth the cost to have the masthead typeset by the printer; otherwise, you should carefully letter it with transfer type.

To begin your layout of the newsletter, take several sheets of heavy, smooth white paper, 8½ by 11 inches in size. Using a nonphoto blue pencil, a T-square, and a triangle, draw lines on the paper to outline your type blocks, gutter, and borders. These blue lines will serve as guides and will not reproduce when the final paste-up, or *mechanical*, is printed. Position your masthead at the top of page one, and glue it down with rubber cement. Be sure to smooth it out, and don't worry if the rubber cement seeps from the edges. When the seepage dries, it can be rubbed away without leaving a trace.

Your copy can be prepared either by typesetting or by typewriting. Typesetting looks better, of course, but typewriting can be just as effective and much cheaper, and can allow you to make changes up to the last minute. If you want to be cost-effective, then, typewriting is definitely the way to go. Use a typewriter with a carbon ribbon (for dark, consistent inking) and a clear typeface, such as IBM's Bookface or Courier. If you need to conserve space, elite spacing (twelve characters per inch) is preferable to pica (ten characters per inch). Using your nonphoto blue pencil on a plain white sheet of paper, draw a column the same size as the type block on your mechanical. Type your copy

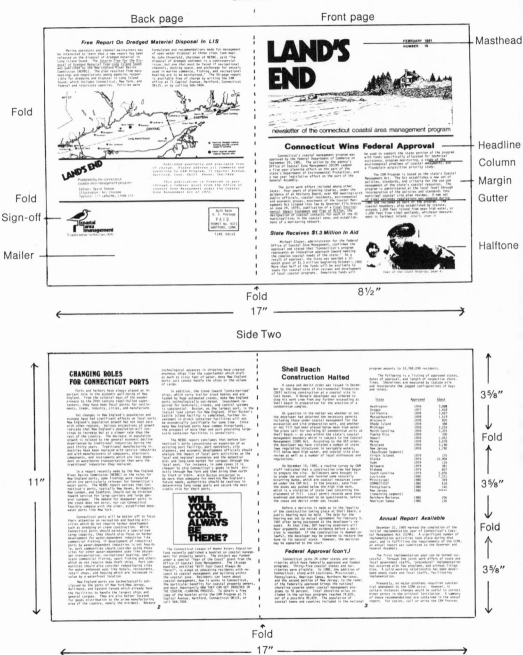

A four-page newsletter. (Courtesy Connecticut Coastal Area Management Program.)

from blue line to blue line, filling the column without exceeding your boundaries. Single-space within paragraphs, and double-space between them. Once all your copy is typed in $3\frac{1}{4}$-inch columns, plan the layout of your newsletter, taking into account text, headlines, halftones (screened photographs), line drawings, and mailing form.

An alternate method of laying out a newsletter, called *reduction printing*, is more commonly used. By having the printer reduce the size of your typescript you can make it look more like typeset copy, and you can accommodate more text in your newsletter. You'll have to type your columns larger; that is, if your printed columns are to be $3\frac{1}{4}$ inches by $9\frac{1}{2}$ inches, and your typescript is to be reduced to 80 percent of original size, type your columns 4 inches by $11\frac{7}{8}$ inches.

Headlines are best set in 18- or 24-point type. You can buy transfer letters in several different faces for variety. The easiest way to develop a sense of headline design, and layout generally, is to examine newspapers and magazines. Headlines can be set either within the $3\frac{1}{4}$-inch column or, if an article is run in two adjacent columns, across both. Letter your headlines on nonphoto graph paper, which can be purchased at most art stores. Before gluing down any text copy, headlines, or illustrations, trim away excess paper, and position everything to fill your pages. Glue your headlines in; then glue in your copy by simply matching the blue lines on your typing page and mechanical.

If you opt to have your newsletter typeset, simply follow the same layout procedure, only instead of typing your copy, give it to a typesetter, who will set it according to your specifications. You will have to determine the typeface, the type size, and the amount of space between lines, known as *leading*. Newsletters are usually set in 8- or 9-point type, with one to three points of leading. The printer will measure the width of your columns in *picas*; there are about six picas in an inch. If your columns are $3\frac{1}{4}$ inches wide, therefore, your lines of type will be $19\frac{1}{2}$ picas long. Specify either 24-point or 18-point type for headlines. After setting the type the printer or compositor will give you *galleys*, or proofs, which you must check for errors. When corrections have been made, you must check the final *repro*, trim it, and lay it out.

Aside from the added cost, the basic drawback to type-setting is the extra time and work it takes to have your copy set, get the galleys back, check them, have corrections made, and lay out the repro. You may also run into problems with deadlines, and you may end up with too much or too little copy. If you need to make last-minute corrections or additions, you will have to go back to the typesetter. Such delays can be bothersome, especially when you are trying to complete the complicated job of getting out a newsletter.

Illustrations—line drawings and photos—can really perk up a newsletter if they are germane and of high quality. Line drawings, which are black and white with no grays, are relatively inexpensive to print. If you know no professional artists willing to donate their time and talent, perhaps you can entice a few art students at a nearby college or high school with a small fee or even just the chance to see their work in print. Have your drawings made to extend across one or two columns, with or without reduction. Have *photostats* (inexpensive photographs produced by a special camera) made from the drawings at the desired size. When you have pasted in the photostats, your newsletter will be camera-ready—that is, ready to be printed.

If you can't get original art, you can instead purchase generic art, or clip art, from art suppliers. *Generic art* refers to uncopyrighted line drawings that are sold in books through most art supply stores. They are usually limited to a special topic, such as flowers, spring, sports, transportation, or buildings. The drawings themselves are simple, much like greeting card art. Any art in the public domain— that is, art on which the copyright has expired or never existed—can be used in the same way. Dover publishes over three hundred volumes of copyright-free art, and most sell for under $5. (A complete catalog is available from Dover Publications, Inc., 180 Varick Street, New York, New York 10014.) The manufacturers of transfer type, such as Letra-set and Chartpak, also offer flourishes, borders, and simple designs, which, if used sparingly, can add appeal to your newsletter. But these are frills—you don't really need them.

Though it is normally too expensive to reproduce color photographs, black and white shots are good attention-getters in newsletters. They should be used sparingly, however, because they are costly and time-consuming to print. As *continuous-tone copy,* a photograph must be shot through a screen to produce a *halftone,* in which the image is broken into thousands of tiny black dots. The benefits of one or two well-placed halftones in a four-page newsletter may justify the added printing costs. Most photographs will need to be cropped and reduced to fit the space available. You should always use a 5-by-7-inch (or larger) black and white glossy print. Crop photos, when appropriate, according to the instructions in Chapter 4.

Next figure how much space you want to give to the photo. If you want to fit a 4-inch wide photo in a 3¼-inch column, use your reduction wheel to find the percentage at which the printer should shoot your photo. Simply line up the original width (4 inches) on the inner disc with the desired width (3¼ inches) on the outer disc. The percentage of original size will appear in the wheel's window; in this case it will be 79 percent.

Keeping the discs thus aligned, find the height of the photo on the inner disc, and note the adjacent measure on the outer disc. This will be the height of the photo when it is reduced. So, if your original photo is 6 inches long and you are reducing it to 79 percent, your printed photo will be 5 inches long.

On your mechanical, indicate in nonphoto blue pencil the size of the printed photo and the percentage at which the printer should shoot the original, in this case 79 percent. On the tissue paper that will cover the photo write, "Reduce to 79%," and identify the photo on both the tissue and the mechanical as, for example, "Photo A." Be sure to leave room on the mechanical for a caption; this can be typed in an italic face and pasted in. Some printers may require that you use blockout paper, or Rubylith, to cover the space intended for each photo. This is an acetate film with a sticky back that can be purchased at an art supply store. After indicating the dimensions of your photo in blue pencil, cut a strip of blockout paper of the same size, peel off the back, and place it on the mechanical. This creates a clear "window" in the negative where the printer will place the half-tone.

If you have more to say than can be accommodated in a four-page newsletter, the page count can easily be increased to six. Instead of an 11-by-17-inch sheet of paper folded once to make four pages, use an 11-by-25½-inch sheet folded twice, in thirds. Because the printer won't have to do any trimming, this is less expensive than including a two-page insert. You can expand to eight pages by using two 8½-by-17-inch sheets, each folded once, with one acting as the insert. The newsletter can be expanded with inserts to a maximum of twelve pages; after that you need some kind of binding. The typical binding for a large newsletter with this format is called *saddle stitching*. Two wire staples are passed through the crease in the newsletter.

Colors can add expense to any publication, but they can also add appeal and help retain the reader's attention. When printing your newsletter you will need to choose at least one color of ink and one color of paper. Even if your budget is tight, you needn't use black ink on white paper. Other colors may cost no more, and they may better highlight your publication. Most printers will be able to offer you a small selection of paper colors, such as green, blue, red, yellow, buff or ivory, beige, white, orange, brown, and gray. The shades vary depending on the paper manufacturer. The important things to remember when considering colors are legibility and mood. The latter quality, of course, is largely subjective. But legibility can be assured, psychological tests show us, with these color combinations:

Black ink on yellow paper

Green ink on white paper

Blue ink on white paper

White on blue paper

Black on white paper

Yellow on black paper

White on red paper

White on orange paper

White on black paper

In a newsletter, any of these combinations will be both attractive and legible: black on any pastel; dark blue on any buff, white, violet, or yellow; dark green on ivory, light green, yellow, or white; and dark brown on beige, light brown, ivory, yellow, tan, or white. Bright colors, obviously, tend to get more attention, but you should be aware that all colors create certain impressions on the reader, both good and bad. Colors such as yellow and red are warm; they seem to move toward the eye. Blue and green are cool; they seem to recede. Red is a bold color that, if used too often, can be overpowering and repelling, whereas blue is associated with water and sky and, as a result, has a kind of spacious or lulling effect. Blue is the best liked of all colors. Green suggests the forest or grass and is also very appealing, whereas purple seems formal (it has always been considered the color of kings), and orange has a burnished quality. Brown appeals to many people; it seems to remind us of wood or leather. Color combinations are infinite, since colors can be blended endlessly to create new shades and new stunning effects. Staying with the basic colors will be less expensive, though. It is important to remember that the right colors help attract and retain attention, create a positive mood, and accentuate your newsletter's message.

Your copy and headlines can be made to appear in white on a dark background through a technique called *reverse printing*. To use this technique you must begin with a white paper stock. The type is *reversed out*—that is, no ink touches the paper where the type is to appear—while the entire background is inked. This can work very effectively when you use a dark color of ink, such as blue or red. It is a good practice to change color combinations (while retaining the same format) with each issue of your newsletter. The colors alone will attract the interest of readers, who will know immediately that they are looking at a new issue.

Before having your newsletter printed, you should also give some thought to distribution—who is to get your newsletter, and how will you send it? Mailing lists and distribution will be discussed in detail in Chapter 9, but it is important to consider them briefly here. An 8½-by-11-inch newsletter can be folded by the printer (or in house to save money) to 8½ inches by 3⅔ inches—a little smaller than a standard business envelope. The newsletter is folded twice, in thirds, just like a letter. In designing your newsletter, leave the bottom third of the last page blank; this is where the recipient's address, your return address, and a first-class stamp or bulk-rate permit number will go. This is very important; it will save you the expense of envelopes, which can be considerable for a large mailing. You should also include a "reverse" heading just above your mailing panel, identifying your group, your editor, and your address; the frequency of publication; and the cost of subscriptions, if any. I also think it wise to include, usually on the last page, a form that readers can clip out and return to tell you if they would like to have their name added to your mailing list, if they would like you to stop sending them the newsletter, or if they have moved. Such a form will save you money by keeping your mailing list up to date. You can either staple the open end of the newsletter or use a sticker to close it. When a stamp is placed in the upper left-hand corner and an address label in the center, the newsletter is ready to be mailed. If your organization is nonprofit, you may be able to mail your newsletter at a special low rate. To do so, you must apply at your local post office for a permit. Special bulk rates, if the newsletters are presorted according to the recipients' addresses, can cut your mailing costs in half.

Handbills

There are two basic designs for handbills, which are printed materials you hand to people as you stand on a street corner, canvass a neighborhood, or introduce your group at a rally or meeting. The text of handbills should be short and simple; they are intended not as sources of comprehensive information but as introductions to your organization and its purpose. They may tell newcomers how they can participate in the organization and where they can get more information, or they may simply announce a rally or important meeting.

A handbill can serve well as a fund-raising device, and, once again, a high-quality publication will create the best impression with prospective donors. The format most commonly used is an 8½-by-11-inch sheet folded twice, in thirds, to 3⅔ inches by 8½ inches. This format is handy; the handbill can be easily slipped into a pocket or pocketbook or into an envelope for mailing. The 3⅔-by-8½-inch format also allows you some interesting design variations, for you have six panels to work with. Both the content and the design must be selected according to the overall purpose and distribution strategy. Before designing the handbill write out exactly what you want to communicate. Try to avoid dates or details that may quickly change and make your handbill outdated and useless. Don't be wordy; use short phrases, or brief paragraphs with simple sentences. Don't pack each panel with copy; your handbill is supposed to address people who have not heard of your group, and most of them will spend no more than two minutes perusing the handbill before deciding whether to keep it or pitch it. (Remember, effective publicity works in a matter of seconds.) And always include your organization's name, logo, address, and phone number so that an interested reader can contact you.

As you design your handbill, consider how the reader will look at it, step by step. Panel 1 should be dramatic and quisitive, almost puzzling; it should make the reader want to look further. Often the reader will look at the back panel, or Panel 2, simply by turning the handbill over. Both Panel 1 and Panel 2 should contain a brief message—a self-explanatory phrase, sentence, or short paragraph—because you don't want to waste the few precious seconds you have to

How can I help?

Post this brochure on a bulletin board in a prominent place such as your grocery store, laundromat or place of employment. It is important for parents under stress to have easy access to our toll-free number.

Use our Speakers' Bureau as a resource for an organization you may belong to or for a local school program. Call 742-7573 for more information about speakers.

Consider becoming a Parental Stress Line volunteer by calling us at 742-7573 and requesting a Volunteer Information Sheet.

Make a tax-deductible donation to the Parental Stress Line. Any amount is appreciated and will assist us in continuing to offer this critically needed program.

Parental Stress Telephone Counseling Service
The Pilot House
Lewis Wharf
Boston, Massachusetts 02110
742-7573 (Business Line)
1-800-632-8188 (Stress Line)

Non-Profit Org.
U.S. Postage PAID
Boston, MA
Permit No. 55171

STOP

Before you do anything
to your child,
do something for yourself!

Call Parental Stress 1-800-632-8188

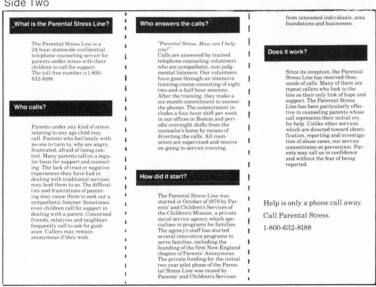

What is the Parental Stress Line?

The Parental Stress Line is a 24-hour statewide confidential telephone counseling service for parents under stress with their children to call for support. The toll-free number is 1-800-632-8188.

Who calls?

Parents under any kind of stress relating to any age child may call. Parents who feel lonely with no one to turn to, who are angry, frustrated, afraid of losing control. Many parents call on a regular basis for support and counseling. The lack of trust or negative experiences they have had in dealing with traditional services may lead them to us. The difficulties and frustrations of parenting may cause them to seek out a sympathetic listener. Sometimes even children call for support in dealing with a parent. Concerned friends, relatives and neighbors frequently call to ask for guidance. Callers may remain anonymous if they wish.

Who answers the calls?

"Parental Stress. How can I help you?"
Calls are answered by trained telephone counseling volunteers who are sympathetic, non-judgmental listeners. Our volunteers have gone through an intensive training course consisting of eight two-and-a-half hour sessions. After the training, they make a six-month commitment to answer the phones. The commitment includes a four-hour shift per week in our offices in Boston and periodic overnight shifts from the counselor's home by means of diverting the calls. All counselors are supervised and receive on-going in-service training.

How did it start?

The Parental Stress Line was started in October of 1979 by Parents' and Children's Services of the Children's Mission, a private social service agency which specializes in programs for families. The agency's staff has started several innovative programs to serve families, including the founding of the first New England chapter of Parents' Anonymous. The private funding for the initial two year pilot phase of the Parental Stress Line was raised by Parents' and Children's Services from interested individuals, area foundations and businesses.

Does it work?

Since its inception, the Parental Stress Line has received thousands of calls. Many of them are repeat callers who look to the line as their only link of hope and support. The Parental Stress Line has been particularly effective in counseling parents whose call represents their initial cry for help. Unlike other services which are directed toward identification, reporting and investigation of abuse cases, our service concentrates on prevention. Parents may call us in confidence and without the fear of being reported.

Help is only a phone call away.
Call Parental Stress.
1-800-632-8188

An 8½-by-11-inch sheet of paper, folded in thirds, makes a simple yet effective handbill that can be easily slipped into a pocket or business envelope. This one is printed in black and red on white paper, with the stop sign reversed out to appear in white on the eye-catching red cover. Rhetorical questions, highlighted with broad red bars, introduce each key point. (Courtesy Parental Stress Telephone Counseling Service.)

make an impression. The handbill is then opened, and the reader is struck by Panel 3 and, to the left, Panel 4. The final layout is the center spread consisting of Panels 4, 5, and 6. Having six panels does not mean that you have to treat each one separately. In fact, a halftone spread across the three inside panels can be very effective; it will seem to leap out as the reader unfolds the handbill. If dramatic enough, it will make a strong impression.

There is no limit to the artistry that can go into a handbill of the double-fold type. I recommend getting a volunteer graphic artist to do the design. Use plenty of line drawings and halftones, and an attractive color combination so the reader will at least *look*, if not *read*. Try to get your copy typeset; since there will be very little, it won't be very expensive if you are charged by the hour. You should have a large number of handbills printed, so that you can use them for several years. Use paper no lighter than 16-pound bond; a 65-pound card stock, though more expensive than bond paper, holds up best.

Handbills are also frequently designed in an even simpler format, at less cost. For this format, a single $8\frac{1}{2}$-by-11-inch sheet of paper is used as is or cut in two, to $8\frac{1}{2}$ inches by $5\frac{1}{2}$ inches. Place a border with your border tape about $\frac{1}{4}$ inch from the edges. With transfer type, letter headlines big and bold to grab the reader's attention, and use a typewriter for the copy (if you have a lot). Place a striking illustration on one side. If you can fit all your information on one side, do so; it will lower your printing costs. Don't fill up every inch of space, and remember to balance your design. Do not use a type block larger than $6\frac{1}{2}$ inches in width and $8\frac{1}{2}$ inches in length, and use reduction printing to improve the appearance of the text. If you have a lot to say, run the copy (with a second headline) onto the reverse side, as you would for a newsletter article. Remember to include your group's name, address, phone number, and logo. Aim to design the handbill with a primary impact like that of a poster, which immediately relays a short message from a distance, and a secondary impact from facts and supporting information, usually on the reverse side.

Handbills should be printed in bright colors, such as canary yellow, or red, or electric blue. You can use a colored ink for contrast if you have them printed, but it is usually cheaper to have them photocopied in black ink on a colored stock. If you opt to have the handbill printed by offset, however, you may consider using reverse printing, with the background in one color of ink and the type in another. The more you print, the lower the cost per copy. If your quantity is large enough (in the thousands, usually), the cost of offset printing will be comparable to the cost of photocopying.

Posters

These are my favorite kind of publication, because a good poster gets lots of attention, allows you to choose from a broad range of images, and can accommodate high art. You need only think of the nineteenth-century posters of Toulouse-Lautrec, which hang in the finest museums today, to appreciate the art form. But you don't have to compete with Toulouse-Lautrec to create an effective poster.

When designing a poster you should first determine what its printed size should be. This will depend on where it will be placed. If you are advertising a performance and want to put a few posters in buildings where there is plenty of space, you can easily accommodate a 22-by-26-inch or 11-by-17-inch format. But if you plan to have your posters plastered around town at bus stations, street corners, and supermarkets, you should probably opt for a size no greater than 11 by 17 inches; 8½ inches by 14 inches or 8½ inches by 11 inches is probably right. The smaller size is most suitable for small (and often cluttered) billboards, telephone poles, and public doorways, to which they can be quickly attached with a staple gun. Whether you'd like your poster to be large or small, you'll lower your printing costs by choosing one of the standard sizes mentioned here.

Posters should not look cluttered; they should catch a viewer's eye and instantly relate a message. A striking illustration, a bold headline, and a few lines telling who, what, where, and when are sufficient. Most of the copy can be let-

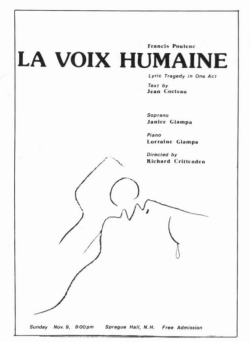

Both of these posters measure 11 by 17 inches. The one at left is printed in black ink on bright blue paper. The name of the opera is emphasized, with supporting information kept to a minimum. The simple sketch attracts the attention of passers-by.

The poster at left is printed in two colors of ink—red for the apple and headline, brown for the rest—on white paper. The bold illustration and bright colors demand attention and instantly transmit the basic message—the coming of a fair. (Courtesy Shady Hill Fair. Design by Shayna Loeffler.)

tered with transfer type, so that typesetting charges can be avoided completely. If you cannot find a graphic artist to volunteer to do a design, keep your poster simple.

Look for a bright colored paper, preferably card stock, and use the legibility guide for handbills to select a color combination. You will probably want to limit yourself to one or two colors of ink; using more may be stretching your budget as well as your talents. Most posters are read from a distance, so legibility is an important factor. If it can't be read from 10 feet away, it doesn't work as a poster. Line drawings work well on posters and are inexpensive to reproduce. If you have a high-quality drawing, you can have the printer enlarge or reduce it as need be; all you will have to do is lay out your transfer type.

If you need to make a very large poster, say 3 feet by 6 feet, you can do so relatively cheaply by cutting a stencil, painting your board a light color such as yellow or white, applying the stencil, and then painting over the stencil with a roller in black or red. This is the method most local politicians use in making the lawn signs that display their names to passers-by. The primary drawbacks of these posters are that sturdy signboards are expensive; you need supporters who will let you place the sign on their property; you need someone with the skill to cut an adequate stencil; you must have the proper tools to cut the boards and stencils and anchor the sign; and you are restricted to one or two words per sign—not enough to make a complex statement. Name recognition is about the most you can accomplish.

Bumper Stickers

These don't tell people a lot about your group, but they help keep your name or cause before the public. If cleverly and tastefully designed, bumper stickers can be handed out like pamphlets or mailed. Their value lies primarily in attracting public recognition to your name or cause. You are obviously very limited in how much you can say on a bumper sticker.

Legibility is a key concern, as it is with posters. In choosing colors, check the legibility guide for handbills. Instead of the standard-sized bumper sticker (5 inches by 14 inches) I like the smaller version (3½ inches by 8 inches). This fits easily in business-size envelopes, as well as on cars and bulletin boards. Whenever you get a request for information on your organization, send a bumper sticker along with such materials as a newsletter and pamphlet. You'll be surprised where they'll end up on display.

There are many more types of publications that you can invest in, of course, but the ones I've discussed here are basic to any successful publicity campaign. The most important thing to remember is that you should put out the best publication you can while sticking to your budget. Neatness, clarity, and legibility all reflect positively on your organization.

In order to get the best publication for your dollar, shop around for a printer who can give you the best service at the lowest price. Some printers specialize in certain types of jobs, and you may need a specialist. Large presses can do almost any job, but they usually charge more because they have a higher overhead. Small printers are generally less expensive and can often find more time to answer your questions. Whichever you choose, be sure the press can deliver a product of adequate quality. Get to know your printer, after you choose one, so you know you can rely on his or her advice. In time you will develop a solid working knowledge of the printing process—from the customer's perspective, at least.

8.

Meeting the Public

PUBLIC speaking is perhaps the oldest form of publicity known to humanity. But though it has been recognized as such for centuries, public speaking still offers unique opportunities to those publicists who dare undertake this time-honored method of influencing people. By dealing with "live" audiences, you can add a personal touch to your publicity campaign that will complement the impersonal techniques of radio interviews, PSAs, and newsletters. By interacting face to face with the individuals you are trying to affect, you can discuss complex issues, answer questions, address special concerns, and win people over. In short, you can get results.

One of the major drawbacks to public speaking is that the number of people it allows you to reach is limited. Even if you draw large audiences as a public speaker, the number of people in attendance can rarely match the number who would see the average TV PSA. Meeting the public inevitably demands large blocks of your time, moreover, particularly if you are making presentations yourself rather than coordinating them. These drawbacks should be weighed carefully before you arrange a speakers bureau or display tour. Consider how much time you can dedicate to these activities, and choose the most appropriate time and place for them.

Public speaking techniques should be used in almost any publicity campaign if adequate resources and opportunities exist. And if you are faced with one of the following circumstances you should consider placing public speaking at the forefront of your campaign.

If your target group is small or clearly defined, you will probably be better off handling the campaign with personal publicity, especially if you or your group is already well known in the community or if the community does not have its own media.

If your issue is highly complex and prone to misrepresentation by the mass media, you may be forced to focus on meetings, seminars, and workshops to get your important points across.

If your audience is made up of young school children or others who do not read or actively listen to radio and television, you should concentrate on personal techniques.

If you are promoting a cause or product, such as an art object, that translates poorly into print or onto television, you may get a better response with live demonstrations or showings.

If your audience is suffering from media overkill, as is likely to happen in a big city, a personal approach may be refreshing, humanizing, and ultimately more effective.

If you are promoting your cause at a fair or rally, you must present your information directly to your audience. You cannot rely on television, radio, or newspapers.

If you are having trouble getting media coverage, a speech by a well-known individual will inevitably draw out reporters.

The Publicist Speaks

You do not have to be a Benjamin Disraeli, Winston Churchill, or Martin Luther King to give an effective talk or presentation. If you can speak like one of them, in fact, I would without hesitation suggest that you give up publicity and go into politics.

It is impossible to tell you precisely what you should or should not say in an oral presentation. The variables are too many. You must take into account your personal abilities and experiences, your opinions, your subject matter, and the format of the talk. If you have little experience in public speaking, I recommend that you get a good handbook (see Chapter 10, "The Publicist's Library") or take a college-level course on the subject. Practice with your friends or fellow workers before entering a campaign centered on public talks.

You will find that public speaking is a personal skill— one that depends on adherence to a set of guidelines known as the Ten Commandments.

1. *Be human.* Use humor and colloquial language, and act natural. Make yourself approachable—like a communicator, not a preacher.

2. *Be prepared*, especially with respect to your subject matter. Know where your talk is going and where you want it to go.

3. *Be enthusiastic.* Show life and energy. Act as though you are truly interested in your subject and enjoy talking to people. Don't drone.

4. *Be confident.* Make people feel that you know what

you are talking about, that you have done your homework, that you are an authority.

5. *Be specific.* Illustrate your points with statistics, quotes, and real-life examples. Supply visual aids where appropriate.

6. *Be accurate.* Make sure that all the information you present is true. Avoid "flying by the seat of your pants," because occasionally you will have an expert in the audience.

7. *Be entertaining.* Add personal interest where possible. Tell stories or anecdotes to illustrate your important points.

8. *Be alert.* Avoid moving through your script like a locomotive down a track. Pay attention to your audience: answer questions fully, clarify all misconceptions, and stay attuned to the general mood of your listeners.

9. *Be relevant.* Make your speech as topical as possible. Relate your themes to local affairs or news events, and show how questions from the audience relate to your important points.

10. *Be calm.* Avoid getting overly nervous. Be friendly; refrain from getting defensive or angry. Communicate physically by smiling, laughing, and dressing neatly. Project an open and receptive personality.

In time you will be able to incorporate the Commandments in your talks. If all this still makes you feel a bit queasy, however, I know a sure-fire way you can make effective presentations without putting yourself on the spot: devise a slide show.

Slide Shows

A slide show consists of a series of 35-millimeter slides projected on a screen to highlight key points of a presentation. As speaker, you control the slide projector while reading from a script. You can stand either in the rear or in the front of the audience, controlling the projector from a switch on an extension cord. With enough practice you will eventually be able to ad-lib while working your projector.

By shifting the audience's attention from the speaker to an image on a screen, slides can really spark up a presentation. They are particularly helpful if the speaker is inexperienced or nervous, or if the subject matter is complex, dull, or technical. A major drawback to using a slide show is that you cannot readily modify it for a specific audience. Another drawback is that you need a properly equipped room (with electrical outlets and curtains to shut out the sunlight) as well as a projector and a screen.

A slide show can be used effectively if you give many talks on the same subject, such as the purpose and scope of your organization or the history of a specific neighborhood. If you will be making a speech more than once, or making several similar speeches, then you can probably justify the expense of time and money required to produce a standard script and accompanying slides. And if several individuals in your organization routinely give talks, they may all be able to use the same slide show, particularly if the central theme of your program can be effectively addressed by this medium.

To begin, state your topic as succinctly as possible. You should be able to sum it up in a single sentence, such as "The goal of Children Without Tears is to help prevent child abuse by bringing about a greater awareness of the problem in our community." Or, "The Save the Wetlands program was started in 1978 to help stop the destruction of our natural resources." Your topic sentence should announce the unifying theme of your slide show.

Second, you should consider the type of audience you will be addressing, and be sure your show suits its lifestyle, economic class, and educational level. Since one of the main reasons for devising a slide show is that you can use it repeatedly, you shouldn't be too limiting. Instead, try to make your slide show appeal to a broad cross section of the population. Explain all concepts and points in easily understood language without sounding simplistic or condescending.

Next, make a list of the key points you would like to make. Devise a structure for your script that is logical, direct, and evenly paced. Give it a beginning, middle, and end. If you are telling the history of your organization, follow the inherent logic of time: start at the beginning, and move chronologically to the most recent events.

Early on, define your subject and explain key concepts and terms. Once your theme has been stated, develop it with examples, secondary points, descriptions, and statistics. In this middle section, be sure to address all your important points. Your ending should sum up the presentation, reiterate your theme, and present logical conclusions.

The right pace for your script is sometimes difficult to determine. *Pace* refers to the timing of the delivery and the intervals devoted to each concept. In many respects, pacing is a personal effect of the speaker. Yet the scriptwriter helps to set the pace by determining the length of sentences and paragraphs. Remember that the script is meant to be spoken and heard; the audience has little time to reflect on what is being said, especially since most of its attention is on the slides. Introduce your main concepts one at a time; refrain from piling them on top of each other. Explain each point; elaborate as necessary; and provide sufficient emphasis. Many of the people in your audience will be hearing these things for the first time, and you want to be certain they follow you. Use colloquial language that is direct and crisp. Avoid convoluted sentences; place your subjects and verbs in easily identified positions.

Once you have drafted the script, read it aloud. If you have trouble pronouncing words, change them. If you cannot read through sentences without pausing for breath, shorten them. Give your script to other members of your group for review. Have different people read it aloud, judging it for smoothness, comprehensibility, and conversational tone. Make sure that everyone, particularly those who are unfamiliar with your subject, understands the script, that concepts are adequately defined, and that key points are justly emphasized. To determine overall length, you should use the word-count guide for radio and television broadcasting: approximately ten seconds for every twenty words.

Visuals. Once you are satisfied with your script it is time to plan your slides. Assuming that you have access to the proper photographic equipment, and to a professional photographer or skilled amateur, start by examining your script and identifying appropriate images. These may include a group of children, trucks moving along a highway, a woman knitting, a flower, or any other picture your words call to mind. If you have written a good script, you will find that nearly every sentence evokes a clear image. Decide which images are most important and which are secondary. You do not want to use so many slides that every couple of seconds a new one must be projected. But neither do you want to have too few slides. A good rule to follow is to have, at maximum, one slide for every fifteen words of script.

Once you have decided on the type and number of slides, you should make a *story-board*. (Graphic arts stores sell pads of paper just for this purpose.) Sketch in each scene you would like to portray (or paste in a magazine photo of a similar scene), and type in the respective portion of your script. In this way you can visualize your presentation and have others review your work before you go to the expense of production. The story-board is also handy in describing your ideas to your photographer, who in viewing it can clearly visualize what you are after. If you use a photographer with some experience, however, it is wise to let that person have as much freedom of interpretation as possible.

Your slides should be in color, clearly focused, and interesting. Avoid posing subjects or trying to illustrate the script too explicitly; you don't want your slides to look phony. Remember, you are trying to add realism to your speech. When selecting your actual slides, look for shots taken at varying angles and depths of field. Choose dramatic action shots—of two runners just about to cross the finish line, for example, or a skier about to launch herself from a ramp. Panoramic shots of landscapes, if relevant, can also work well, as can topographical shots of cities, coastlines, and mountains. But you shouldn't get carried away with the grandeur of panoramic shots. Instead, emphasize objects and, especially, people—always try to add the human touch.

Look for natural groupings among your slides. You might plan a sequence of contrasting scenes—a particular spot in a forest photographed in summer, perhaps, followed by a shot of the same spot in winter, or a shot of a heavily urbanized area accompanied by a shot of a rural setting. Historical shots also work well; you might show a slide made from an old photo of a certain neighborhood, and follow it with a shot of the same scene today. If you are trying to show progression, concentrate on the logical sequence of events. For example, say you want to show a group of boy scouts cleaning up the debris in a local brook. You might identify this natural sequence and portray it with slides:

The debris-laden brook

A group of boy scouts getting instructions

The boys approaching the brook

The boys (or a boy) removing various debris

The boys removing debris (a different shot)

The boys loading debris in a truck

The boys smiling near a clean brook

The cleaned-up brook at sunset

Try not to use too many sequences; when used in excess they begin to look stale and slow down the presentation. Whereas sequences are descriptive, contrasts are dramatic.

Word and graphic slides make up a special category of visuals. A word slide is simply a color or black and white shot of an address, phone number, or list. Word slides are good for displaying important addresses or emphasizing key points, but because they are not very interesting or attractive, they should be used sparingly. An example of a graphic slide would be a shot of your group's logo. When placed among action shots, word and graphic slides provide a change of pace and call attention to special points in your slide show.

Varying the type of slides is one way to alter pace and add drama; spacing your slides is another way. You can indicate spacing for the speaker by placing sequential numbers, one for each slide, at appropriate points in the text. Try to avoid placing them too regularly—every fifteen words, for example, or at the beginning of every sentence. Show some slides in quick succession, and others slowly with greater explanation. Give more time and emphasis to those slides that are especially interesting or complex. Whereas a sequence of action shots, as in my boy scout example, might be shown quickly, slides showing historical contrasts or topographical scenes would require more time and explanation. Varying the intervals between slides will prevent monotony; the viewer never knows what to expect next.

Once your slide show is prepared, you needn't always follow your script word for word. A certain amount of ad-libbing can be very effective, in fact, especially as you become more familiar with your slides and your subject matter, and more confident. Ask rhetorical questions during the presentation to encourage audience participation. Invite the audience to raise questions; explain slides to which people react strongly; and tell anecdotes. In time you will have a store of ad-libs for nearly every slide. By varying points of emphasis you can tailor your slide show to the interests of each audience and break the glaze of a prepared talk.

You can increase your flexibility even more by substituting slides, or even series of slides. Or you can simply add or delete certain slides to slant your presentation. A deletion may be as simple as removing two slides that have become outdated or are not particularly relevant to your audience. You might develop a whole file of slides for possible addition, or even several ten-minute mini–slide shows that illustrate certain aspects of your program in depth. As you become more experienced you will find yourself adapting like a chameleon to changing conditions. I know of no better way to develop skill and confidence in public speaking than working with slides. If properly designed, a slide show can bring out the best in almost any speaker.

Speakers Bureaus

A speakers bureau is no more than a pool of speakers who speak in public as representatives of your organization. They may be staff members, club members, directors, or volunteers with particular expertise. A speakers bureau can have as few as two speakers—your club president and yourself, for instance. Assuming that you are both capable speakers, all you need to do is offer your services, free of charge, to schools, groups, and clubs. You can publicize your bureau through your newsletter and various other channels such as PSAs, telephoning, and direct mail. Depending on the amount of interest your topic has, you will inevitably get requests—perhaps more than you can handle —from Rotary Clubs, neighborhood organizations, schools and colleges, symposiums, and the like.

Set up your bureau this way: for each member who is willing to occasionally speak, make a small file, including area of expertise, personal interests or hobbies, affiliations, availability, experience, and a brief biography. Based on the information in your completed files, make a list of possible topics for talks. When publicizing your bureau, stress that you are prepared to supply any of several speakers, whose combined expertise covers a range of topics. (You should not claim your speakers as experts, of course, unless they really are.) Emphasize also that your talks can be tailored to suit the interests of a particular audience.

When you get a request for a speaker, refer to your list of possible topics. If your caller has no specific topic in mind, you can suggest one; at the same time you will know you can offer a speaker who can talk effectively on the topic. Occasionally callers will have a topic in mind that is not directly related to your cause; in this case you should diplomatically suggest one your bureau can better handle.

Before proposing any topic, find out the nature of the organization sponsoring the talk; the number of people expected to attend; and their ages, general backgrounds, and affiliations. You should also learn why the organization is sponsoring the talk (is it part of an annual meeting?); whether other speakers are involved; the time, location, and desired length of the talk; and how the organization heard about your bureau. This information will help you gauge the expectations and interests of the prospective audience. You would not want to talk over the heads of a high school audience; nor would you want to sound condescending before an adult audience. With an audience that comprises a broad range of ages, educational levels, and experiences, it can be difficult to focus a talk. Such an audience must be treated with care; the talk should be sufficiently encompassing to interest everyone.

Confirm the topic (place and time, too) with the sponsor only after you have spoken to members of the speakers bureau. This will allow you to make changes or back out altogether if you cannot get a suitable speaker.

Featured Speakers

Any group can win great attention by engaging a well-known person to speak in its name. A "big name" speaker can attract a large audience to your presentation, add to your group's credibility, and provide a peg for your publicity. No matter where you live, you can probably find a few recognized individuals willing to get on a soap box. They may feel strongly about an issue, or they may participate as a civic duty. Robert Redford, for example, has a reputation for coming out in support of certain environmental causes. The featured speaker needn't be someone nationally known, like Henry Kissinger, Jesse Jackson, Gloria Steinem, or Jacques Cousteau, although any of these individuals would be a publicity powerhouse. You will have better luck enlisting local personalities, such as the mayor, state legislators, religious leaders, state and city commissioners, professors, authors, newspaper editors and reporters, and television and radio hosts. State and local politicians are particularly receptive to such requests, but you might use almost anyone who is recognized and respected in your community.

Be sure to explain to any potential speaker that you are looking for a volunteer, because many expect honorariums for their services. You may approach the potential speaker this way:

> Dr. Polly Anna, my organization, Hemlock Citizens for Poison Control, is sponsoring a series of talks by well-respected members of Hemlock. We are trying to pro-mote environmental safety and raise the community's awareness concerning the amount of poisons to which our children are exposed every day. Your being a prom-inent physician in Hemlock, we were hoping that we could sign you up for a brief talk on a related subject of your choice. We have already signed up. . . .

Give as much detail as the potential speaker asks for.

Once the speaker agrees to participate, follow up with a letter reiterating the time, place, and topic agreed on, and offer any services, such as graphic preparation, that you are prepared to render. Make the job of the speaker, who is probably a very busy person, as easy as possible. At the presentation itself, quietly take credit for making the engagement; you will benefit by association. Guard against monopolizing the event: just provide the backdrop, grease the skids, and let your speaker run away with the show. Otherwise the speaker may feel used, and the audience may find your group annoying. Word will get around, and other potential speakers may decline your invitations to speak at future events.

Panel Discussions

A panel discussion is an elaborate version of the featured speaker's talk. Three or four speakers are used, and instead of focusing on a narrow topic they discuss several issues. The result is likely to be a thorough examination of your general subject from diverse perspectives.

Because the discussion will be especially stimulating if

the panelists have opposing views, you should select speakers with different opinions or areas of expertise. If you were sponsoring a discussion on your state's property tax policies, for instance, you might enlist a pro speaker, a con speaker, and a moderate. You would avoid choosing people with the same affiliation, such as several members of the state legislature; because they would already know one another's views well, they would probably give a lackluster performance. You might instead engage a state representative, a local official such as the town assessor or town manager, a spokesperson from a local property owner's association, and a representative of a local building association or renters' union. This way you would be sure to get different opinions, and a lively discussion touching on many issues concerning property taxes. You would also be likely to get a healthy cross section of the public in your audience.

The conventional panel discussion always includes a moderator. He or she should be an important person—or at least should seem important. To ensure visibility for your organization, try to place one of your members in this role. The moderator opens the discussion and introduces the panelists. After each panelist gives a brief spiel, typically, the discussion is open to questions and comments from the moderator and the audience. The moderator poses questions, prepared in advance, when the discussion starts to drag, and can be especially helpful when arguments get heated.

If your topic does not lend itself well to an open discussion, you can opt to have panelists formally address a predetermined topic, with no intervening questions or discussion. This allows the audience to hear several fifteen- to twenty-minute talks. Heated arguments are avoided, and the moderator (if there is one) need only be certain that the program stays on track. Questions should be taken, however, after all participants have had their chance to speak.

Seminars and Workshops

Holding a seminar or workshop is another way of examining issues in depth before the public. Although much like a panel discussion, a seminar or workshop places more emphasis on audience participation and learning. The typical seminar or workshop involves several speakers or teachers with different affiliations and areas of expertise. Each holds a class on a specific, predetermined topic. Participants thus learn about each issue from an expert; they can exchange ideas, raise questions and concerns, and generally gain insight into the issue's significance. They may even engage in role playing.

Most seminars and workshops begin with opening remarks from a sponsor—your president, perhaps—who introduces the leaders and participants. Participants can sign up for several classes, which run throughout the day or weekend. Coffee and lunch breaks encourage socializing and informal exchanges of information.

In setting up a seminar or workshop you may benefit from the help of experienced teachers, who can set realistic schedules. Be sure to balance the topics and to select leaders with diverse backgrounds. Though a seminar or workshop does not enable you to reach a great number of people directly, it provides an opportunity to work with key individuals in other organizations. They may in turn offer support for your cause through their own activities and membership.

Whether you choose to sponsor a featured speaker program, a panel discussion, or a seminar or workshop, you must make certain preparations. First, you should enlist qualified speakers—with public-speaking experience, expertise, character, reliability, and appeal. Second, make sure your speakers and participants represent a broad cross section of the populace. Third, secure adequate facilities—such as a library, high school, or office headquarters—well in advance, and arrange dates and times most convenient for the intended audience.

Fourth, plan a program that is both entertaining and informative. No one wants to sit in a hot, crowded room for three hours while a speaker drones. Keep your lectures brief; break up each presentation with interesting visuals, such as slides or a short film; and allow for questions from the audience. Fifth, make sure you'll have sufficient attendance, even if you have to bring your family or get your members to attend by holding your monthly organizational meeting just prior to the talk. Nothing will discourage your speakers—and any reporters present—as a half-empty hall will. If you are unsure how large the turnout will be, reserve a modest-sized room; it's better to have people standing in the aisles than a lot of empty chairs.

Sixth, announce the event through all established publicity outlets. Not only will you get coverage in your newspaper's community calendar, but you may also get reporters to attend. Be sure your newsletter announces the event (perhaps even do a follow-up article), and make sure your members are aware of the event.

Information Booths and Displays

Two types of displays can be used for publicity. One is the floor display, which stands in a lobby, exhibition hall, or storefront window. The other is the information booth, which differs from a floor display in one major way: it requires people to run it. Although only one of these displays involves public speaking, I have included them both here because well-designed materials can be used in either circumstances.

There are literally hundreds of different designs for displays, ranging from the super-duper, electronically controlled, computer-programmed models used by large businesses to the makeshift boards and panels you see at small, local outdoor fairs and bazaars. To be effective, displays need not be fancy or expensive, only portable. As mobile advertisements, their purpose is to reach a crowd where other publicity methods are inadequate. Information booths offer publicists a particular advantage: they allow you to be the sole source of information on a topic at a fair or exhibition. You can talk directly to the public, presenting facts and answering questions—a persuasive way to publicize an event, cause, or organization.

When planning your display, the most important quality to keep in mind is simplicity. Having spent a lot of time on the environmental fair circuit, I cannot stress enough the benefits of a display that can be put together and taken apart easily and quickly. At a weekend-long exhibition you may have to set up and break down your display three or four times. And if you lose or break a part, you'll be in trouble.

Another important quality to plan for in your display is flexibility. Now I don't mean that the materials should be pliable, but that your display should be easy to set up in a variety of positions and locations. A booth measuring 7 feet by 5 feet, for example, will serve well if you are allotted at least 8 feet by 6 feet of display space. But exhibition directors won't concern themselves with the dimensions of your booth; most simply divide the available area into equal parts. Too bad if your display doesn't fit. And since most exhibitors think nothing of stealing part of their neighbor's allotted space to accommodate their oversized displays, you may arrive to find your space even tighter than the rest. Or you may be assigned a corner space with an I-beam in the center. You should plan a display that can be adapted easily in such situations.

The third quality to look for in a display is durability. Display booths take a lot of abuse in transit, during setup and breakdown, and when crowds descend upon them. Buy flimsy materials only if you plan to use the display no more than once. Durability is especially important when exhibitions are held outdoors, where you have to compete against winds and occasional rainstorms.

Fifth, your display should be attention-getting. Bright banners, large posters and signs, and even sound tracks are appropriate. Smaller items—booklets, pamphlets, sign-up sheets for further information, photos, posters, or other materials that browsers can casually examine—should also be attractively presented.

You will need a table (which is often supplied by the organizers of the exhibition), two chairs for those working the booth (also usually supplied by the organizers), a large tablecloth, at least two panels (which you will have to construct), and a banner. The tablecloth should cover the surface of a 7-by-3-foot table and reach the floor at the front and sides. The material should be durable and a very bright color—like royal blue, orange, yellow, or red—to grab the attention of passers-by. Your banner, on which should appear simply the name of your organization or cause, should be about 6 feet long and 9 inches wide. It can be inexpensively constructed of very light canvas, with a smooth coating of white paint, and stenciled with bold, dark letters. Once dry, it can be rolled up for easy transport. You can staple or pin it to the front of the tablecloth, or you can attach it to a styrofoam board which should be in turn attached to the table.

The panels are a bit more difficult to construct. Each should be approximately 7 feet high and 2½ feet wide, on a frame of two-by-twos, or even two-by-fours for greater strength. Cut two 7-foot lengths and two 26-inch lengths for each panel. Nail them together at the corners, and bind them with metal corner hinges. Next, take a sheet of ¼-inch plywood, pegboard, or even paper-covered styrofoam, measuring 4 feet by 2½ feet, and nail or glue it to the upper portion of the frame. Spray-paint the entire panel, once again with a very bright color to get attention. Then join each pair of panels with small door hinges so the display can be opened and closed. Cut a beam approximately 4 feet long, and drill holes in both ends. Screw the ends of the beam into the bottom front corners of the frame. It will keep the display erect as long as you'd like, and you can detach it to collapse the display for transport. For extra support you can place a weight of some type on the crossbeam; this may be necessary at an outdoor exhibition, where a sudden gust of wind could cause a disaster.

Once you have assembled the panels you must decide what you want to display on them. The simplest yet most effective displays make use of color photos. If your group is concerned about nuclear proliferation, for example, you might display an enlarged photo of the infamous mushroom cloud; if you are concerned with the depletion of water re-

An information booth with two pairs of display panels. Each panel, constructed on a frame of two-by-twos or two-by-fours, is approximately 7 feet high and 2½ feet wide. A support beam screwed into the bottom outside corners holds the 'panels erect. A booth like this might be set up at a fair or exhibition, with a group representative present to answer questions from passers-by. The panels could also be erected without table, chairs, or anyone in attendance as a floor display in a lobby, hall, or window.

sources in the Southwest, then you might display pictures of dry creek beds. If you are promoting a human service, such as a drug rehabilitation clinic, simply show close-up photos of people, preferably staff and patients. All photos used in a display should measure at least 8-by-10 inches and be in color. Like the cover of a magazine, they are meant to grab the viewer's attention. Dry-mount them on styrofoam boards and trim them. Stick them to the face of the panels with styrofoam tape so that they can be removed or replaced as needed.

Each side of the panel can easily accommodate three 8-by-10-inch photos. This will leave enough room for captions, which may concern the photos specifically or your program in general. If you were making a display for the drug rehabilitation clinic, for instance, you might place three photos of staff and patients on each panel. Between the photos you would place captions, each a line or two long and in large letters, to be easily read from several feet away. Your captions might read something like this:

The Bakersfield Drug Rehabilitation Clinic was founded in 1976.

Since that time we have helped over 200 persons with chronic drug problems.

Our staff of trained physicians, psychiatrists, and counselors have many years of experience and are committed to the care of our patients.

On the second panel you would have three more photos and captions:

The clinic, located at the corner of Vine and Day streets, is open 24 hours each day.

Treatment and counseling is free and strictly confidential.

If you have a drug-related problem, or know someone who does, stop in or give us a call at 222-1000.

The captions can be either typewritten or transfer-lettered, and enlarged by a printer so the capital letters are about 2 inches high. Like the photos, the captions may be dry-mounted on styrofoam boards, which are then attached to the face of the panel, and easily removed, replaced, or updated as the need arises.

You can even go as far as putting together different displays, or even duplicates, that can be erected at two or more locations simultaneously.

Even in places where an information booth cannot be accommodated, your segmented, collapsible display may be. When it is not being used in a formal exhibition, erect it in a lobby, storefront window, or hallway, at your headquarters or elsewhere. At all times, your display can serve as an inexpensive, untroublesome publicity tool.

Running an Information Booth

Your newly constructed display can be a valuable publicity

tool at craft shows, fairs, and local rallies. Whenever you hear about such an affair, get in touch with the coordinator and ask if your information booth can be included. Most fairs charge exhibitors a slight fee, but they will almost always make an exception for a nonprofit organization representing a public benefit. Since most such events occur annually, once you have attended a number of them you will find that you have become part of a display circuit. In time you will be invited to more events than you can attend.

In running your display booth, there are certain techniques that should be used in dealing with the public. Always have newsletters, brochures, and other printed materials available. They can be displayed on your table with a small sign saying, "Take one, free of charge." Other items popular at exhibitions are posters. I strongly recommend giving away attractive, well-designed posters; they draw people like magnets. And they continue to give your group attention when the exhibition is over; you may later find them displayed in offices, schools, and homes. You should also provide a sheet or postcards for people to sign if they'd like their name placed on your mailing list.

To create the best impression, be sure to dress neatly. Remember, you represent your organization and are a direct reflection on it. Be prepared to talk to people as they come by, but refrain from giving them the hard sell. It is often best to smile passively as people browse; otherwise you may scare some away. Most people at exhibitions are only mildly interested in the displays. They may pass hundreds, and they don't want to be harangued by everyone with a booth. Let your panels and your literature do the talking. If people are interested they will read your panels; when they are finished, simply greet them and offer a newsletter or brochure. If they have questions they will probably ask.

You will probably end up answering the same questions over and over again. Try to be friendly and personable, and answer directly. Occasionally you may be intimidated by an "expert"—someone who knows far more than you about your subject—but they are rare.

Many fairs and exhibitions are covered by newspapers,

radio, and television, so be prepared to talk to reporters. Know why your group is sponsoring the booth and what the exhibition is all about. Usually reporters will want a quote or two about your organization: its purpose, membership, and location. And occasionally they will ask your opinion of the exhibition.

Your purpose in running an information booth is to gain recognition, maintain visibility, and sign people up for your mailing list; you should focus on these basic publicity goals. Though exhibitions will not give you the opportunity to discuss issues in depth, they will give you experience in responding to a wide range of people quickly and effectively —an important skill for the practical publicist.

9.

Networking

A GRASS-ROOTS method of reaching the public, networking makes the most out of meager resources. Developed in the sixties and seventies to support the anti-war protests and later the environmental movement, networks have been used successfully for fund raising, political organizing, and publicity. Perhaps the most familiar networks are those used by politicians, who enlist so-called foot soldiers to do the laborious jobs of canvassing, telephone soliciting, and posting bills. You can adapt these same inexpensive methods in your campaign to make effective use of club members, volunteers, and other organizations. Though it can be time-consuming and frustrating, networking can also produce considerable public attention and support.

In a broad sense, networking is simply the strategy of capitalizing on unity and alliance. By enlisting the help of many individuals, who may not have the skills to contribute to your campaign on their own, you can orchestrate an out-pouring of information and support that will saturate a community. In a more restricted sense, however, the word *networking* refers to specific techniques for winning support, for making an issue hotter than it currently is, and for making an organization seem large and powerful. Specific networking techniques can enable you to draw on the resources and experiences of existing organizations to boost a fledgling or faltering campaign.

Networking should supplement your regular activities, not replace them. It is difficult to establish an effective network unless the community is already aware of your cause or your organization, since most people are unwilling to volunteer their services for an unfamiliar cause. But networks are a natural outgrowth of a vigorous publicity campaign. The networking techniques presented here include those that are standard and others so simple that even the most modest-sized groups could use them effectively. They include coalitions, petition drives, canvassing, film libraries, mailing lists, and phone trees.

Coalitions

A coalition is a temporary alliance of individuals and organizations with a common goal, such as passing a legislative bill, opposing a city's development policies, supporting a teachers' strike, or backing a nuclear arms freeze resolution. Many lobbyists on the state and federal level, as well as legislators, grass-roots organizers, labor unions, school teachers, professional societies, and other groups, are active in forming coalitions. Technically, a coalition can have as few as two members, as long as they represent different groups. But the most effective coalitions include as many members as possible.

To form a coalition, start by clearly defining your goal in writing. Even before you get members, settle on an image for your coalition by giving it a name, such as Friends of Cleveland, Citizens for a Crime-Free City, or Small Businesses for Tax Reform. Then put out an open invitation to prospective members—specifically, those organizations and individuals who would be particularly instrumental in reaching your goal. Your invitation will be most effective if sent by mail and followed up with a personal phone call. Include a date, time, and place for your first organizational meeting, and, to encourage a large turnout, stress the fact that those attending will be under no obligation to join.

At the organizational meeting you will want to cover certain ground rules. Make introductions, define your basic goals, and elect a chairperson. Your chairperson should be an experienced and capable leader who represents an established or well-regarded group. Try to avoid being elected chairperson yourself—your aim is to encourage outside participation. Those attending should be encouraged to offer suggestions concerning the coalition's basic goals, whether or not a coalition of this type can be effective, potential strategies for accomplishing your goal, and potential contributions of each affiliate. You should also set a life span for the coalition; people will feel more comfortable joining if they know they won't have to attend monthly meetings *forever*. You may want to act as coalition secretary, taking minutes, scheduling and coordinating meetings, receiving and distributing correspondence, and keeping members informed. Since you have proposed the formation of the coalition, you should be prepared to make it easier for others to participate by taking an active role in the administrative chores.

Once the ground rules have been established you can begin to talk seriously about strategy. The coalition's strategy should be formulated collectively, with each member participating as actively as possible. Don't dictate policies; rather, try to incorporate the range of resources, opinions, and ideas of those present. Make a list of tasks and distribute it to all. Tasks should be evenly divided among coalition members, and they shouldn't be complicated, difficult, or overly time-consuming. Remember that participants in the coalition are not your employees; they all have many other daily chores. They should be able to perform coalition tasks in the course of their regular duties. If someone puts out a newsletter, for example, that person might have the task of including an article on your cause. Tasks may be as general as talking to reporters about the issue, running stories in publications, discussing the issue at club meetings, and writing a letter to an influential person or group. Your aim is to get people interested in your cause so they will advance it through their own established networks. (Keep in mind that many members may expect you to help their campaign when the time comes; you should make an effort to reciprocate.) Through coalition participants you may gain access to several newsletters, membership networks, mailing lists, and meetings. You may find your issue getting press coverage from unexpected sources. A rally may be held at city hall or the state capitol; posters may appear promoting the issue; and volunteers may start canvassing neighborhoods. What more could you ask for?

Even though most coalition members can promote your cause on their own, it is important to hold regularly scheduled progress meetings and continually solicit new members. Maintain open lines of communication, and make each member feel like an important force behind your campaign. Try to make the coalition itself well-known by publicizing its formation, membership, and efforts. Even if your members generate less publicity than expected, the coalition's existence can provide material for articles and news releases that emphasize the broad-based support your cause enjoys. The formation of a coalition will increase public awareness and acceptance of your cause.

Mobilizing Membership

Persons directly involved with your organization—as directors, members, or employees—are valuable resources in your publicity campaign. Try to involve them in all publicity activities, even if they can participate only marginally.

If your organization does not currently offer paid memberships, you might consider starting up a membership drive. You need not obligate members to do anything except fill out a brief application form and pay small dues. In turn, you will grant them the right to take part in club activities or simply receive newsletters and other informative materials in the mail. As your members increase, be sure to print their names in your newsletter and release a membership count to the press. Even if your members remain relatively inactive, make sure that reporters, politicians, and other organizations know that you represent them. When you have a dues-paying constituency people take notice—both the press and the public begin to view your activities with greater interest.

Besides helping you create and build a public image, members can also be used directly in publicity activities. As they receive your mailings—including newsletters, brochures, minutes of meetings, fact sheets, and white papers—your members will become your informed constituency. Inevitably, as they talk to friends and family about your cause, they will serve as a powerful though informal publicity force. Through other organizations to which they belong, they may locate opportunities for you to speak, to attend exhibitions, and to establish coalitions.

Your members also constitute a cadre of interested citizens who can be mobilized in times of crisis or at crucial points in a campaign, like two days before the town council votes on an important issue. They will often respond to requests for support at rallies and meetings, and some may take part in your lobbying efforts. As your organization's foot soldiers, they may phone or write legislators, solicit new members, and form committees to address certain problems or accomplish specific tasks.

Using members for a letter-writing campaign can be a particularly effective way to publicize an issue or exert pressure. If you wanted to discourage the editor of your local daily from allowing biased reporting on a certain issue, a hundred or so letters from your members would really get that editor's attention. Letter-writing campaigns often succeed in forcing politicians and government officials, particularly on the state and local level, to address specific issues.

In any letter-writing campaign you should brief your members on the key points to be made, and then instruct them to send personal letters, preferably on their own stationery. Letters make the strongest impression when they are handwritten in the sender's own words; a pile of form letters seems much less the product of sincere individual efforts. Even if you fail to sway them, the people who receive your letters will at least become aware of your organization, your cause, and your active membership.

Occasionally you will have to mobilize your membership rapidly—the night before an important rally or meeting, for example. If you happen to have several hundred members, reaching them becomes difficult unless you have established a phone tree. A phone tree works on the principle of the chain letter: each member takes the names and phone numbers of two others. To activate the system you simply call the two people at the base of the tree, relay the message, and instruct them to call their contacts. They call two other members, who in turn call two more—and so on, until all members have been contacted. The cost of this method is negligible, and you will be surprised to learn how quickly two people multiply into two hundred.

Petitions and Endorsements

A petition drive can generate an avalanche of support, particularly if you use it to win endorsements. A petition is no more than a list of signatures that attests to the support of its signers for a specific cause; it is used to show that a percentage of the populace shares a certain opinion. Such percentages are meaningful in a democratic society, where the will of the people supposedly rules. Petitioning the government is a right—but if you wish your petition to be recognized you must adhere to the rules of your particular jurisdiction. All signers may have to be of a specific political party, for instance; they may have to reside in a specific area; or their signatures may have to be legible and certified. The number of signatures you will need also varies, depending on the issue. Sometimes you may need a specific number for your petition to be recognized; other times you'll want to get as many as possible. Before starting any petition drive you should make sure that you fully understand all the rules that apply. If your petition is aimed at state officials, check with your state secretary. If it is addressed to city officials, contact your city hall.

A statement of your cause should head your petition, for all signers to read. If you are circulating a petition calling for a ban on further nuclear development, then your heading might read:

> I support a ban on nuclear energy in the city of Atomville and urge Mr. Mayor, and the town council, to enact an ordinance prohibiting further development within city limits.

When you approach potential signers—on the street, at a rally, or on the doorsteps of their homes—simply make a brief statement and ask them to sign. Whether they sign or say no, just thank them and leave. Don't try to badger them into signing or "educate" them on the spot. And if they refuse don't take it personally.

When people agree to sign, make sure they include the appropriate information, and then read it aloud to be sure it is legible. If they seem interested in your cause but are uncommitted, describe your organization briefly, explain what you are trying to accomplish, and offer a brochure. You might also put them on your mailing list.

Once you've obtained all the signatures you need and your petition is certified, deliver it in person to the appropriate official. Make sure that you issue press releases well in advance so any interested reporters can attend your presentation. The purpose of the petition is to encourage the official, if sympathetic, to speak out publicly in support of your cause. In the case of opponents, petitions may encourage them to tone down their opposition. As long as your cause isn't highly controversial, most politicians will jump at the chance to curry favor with some voters. At the very least, your petition will make them aware of your group, your purpose, and the fact that your cause has considerable public support.

If you can get the official to make a public statement in

support of your cause—or to declare a day in support of it—
reporters can cover the endorsement. Once they do, remind
the press about your cause frequently, feature the endorsement in your newsletter, invite the official to speak on the
subject, and keep him or her on your mailing list. You can
get a lot of mileage out of such an endorsement; the bigger
the name, the more mileage you will get.

When the late Governor Ella Grasso of Connecticut once
endorsed a campaign I was working on, we managed to create a wave of publicity based on her support. In fact, a petition of only 250 signatures, gathered by a local coalition,
had prompted the governor to issue her official endorsement.
Governor Grasso never even made a public announcement;
one of her press agents wrote the proclamation, which des-
ignated 1980 the "Year of the Coast" in Connecticut and ex-
tolled the virtues of Connecticut's coastline. The governor
simply signed it, and the official seal was applied. The press
agent, knowing that I handled publicity for the state's
Coastal Management Program, sent me the proclamation in
late December 1979.

The governor's declaration for Connecticut followed
President Carter's declaration for the nation. And although
the governor's statement didn't mention the Coastal Man-
agent Program itself, it alluded to issues key to our campaign. So I wrote this press release:

Governor Grasso Declares 1980 "Year of the Coast"

Governor Ella Grasso declared today that 1980 would be des-
ignated the "Year of the Coast" in Connecticut. "I am proud
to designate 1980 as the Year of the Coast," she said, "in
recognition of the innumerable ways in which our coastal resources have shaped our history and their vital influence on
the future of our state and nation."

"This year, the United States government is sponsoring
a special observance to expand public awareness of the need
for careful supervision of our coastal resources. This important initiative is an excellent means of assuring the protection of our shoreline and a timely reminder of its significance
in our region," she said.

The action comes in the wake of a presidential designation for the nation and is particularly fitting for Connecticut because 1980 marks the start of implementation of the state's Coastal Area Management Program, with federal approval expected sometime during the same year.

Arthur Rocque, manager of the state's program, felt that the designation was indeed appropriate. "In terms of initiatives to help conserve coastal resources, 1980 will mark the greatest step forward for Connecticut," he said.

The Coastal Management Act, which Governor Grasso signed into law last June, becomes effective January 1, 1980. Workshops were held in December on the CAM program to acquaint state and municipal officials with their responsibilities under the act. And more workshops are anticipated throughout the year. "On the municipal level, the workshops were aimed at informing local officials and at showing them the range of technical assistance available," Rocque said. They covered such topics as mapping the local boundary, identifying critical resources, and methods for reviewing coastal site plans.

"In many respects, the degree of success Connecticut's program does achieve will depend on the action taken by the municipalities," Rocque added. Under Connecticut's act, coastal towns each receive an initial $2,500 for start-up costs of implementing coastal management. Additional funds are scheduled to become available later in the year to help local municipalities in further planning for the protection of their shorelines. As Governor Grasso put it, "Controlling erosion, flooding and pollution of our coast is a concern that will require the skill and cooperation of all our people in the years ahead." *

My release linked the governor's statement with the activities of the Coastal Area Management Program. I quoted the governor's remarks, and followed them with a statement by our manager concerning our program and the coastal legislation that had been recently signed into law. I sent the release, along with a copy of the governor's proclamation, to about forty media contacts four days before the new year.

Publicity poured in. Dozens of newspapers ran stories based on the release, and radio stations described the desig-

* Reprinted with permission of the Coastal Area Management Program, Connecticut Department of Environmental Protection.

nation as the state's way of ringing in the new year. Months later magazines and newsletters were still running quotes from the release. Several television stations ran stories on the Year of the Coast, and the state's largest station ran a week-long series of reports on the coastal legislation. We were amazed at what just 250 signatures had done. But they hadn't done it alone—one other signature, that of the Grand Lady Governor of Connecticut, had added great weight to ours.

Volunteers

Smart publicists know that most medium-sized cities have a special source of free publicity—the local university or college. College students, particularly those with skill in writing, graphics, or photography, can make contributions of professional quality to your publicity campaign. There are two basic ways to attract student volunteers. The first is to ask the appropriate academic department if it offers an internship program, in which students can earn academic credit while employed in their field of study. If such a program is available, then simply request a student with the needed skills. One will be assigned for a certain period of time, usually no more than three or four months. Though still in school, your intern will have considerable expertise you can put to work in producing articles, newsletters, slide shows, and other materials. Students benefit from internships by gaining work experience which can possibly help them land a job after graduation. And you'll be offering the intern a chance to try out skills acquired in the classroom in a real-life setting. Ideally, an internship offers mutual benefits to the student and the sponsoring organization.

The second way to enlist student volunteers is to devise a project that can be completed without your supervision. This might be building and designing a display booth, producing a slide show, designing a newsletter or poster, or writing and illustrating an information booklet. After defining the project, ask the instructor of a journalism or graphic arts class if some of the students might be willing and able to help, either collectively or individually. You may be able to enlist a couple of students—say a writer and an artist—who can collaborate on the project.

Journalism students are often especially eager to build their portfolios by writing for newspapers and newsletters. You might arrange with your local newspaper to plan a supplement on a specific topic, then ask journalism students to write several articles for it. The students will be rewarded with publication; the newspaper editor will get free reporting; and you'll get plenty of publicity and in-depth treatment of your issue.

High school students should not be overlooked as potential sources for volunteer help, though you should probably refrain from having them undertake any tasks that require great skill, such as writing or illustrating. They can best be employed as foot soldiers—to turn out in mass to help stuff mailboxes, to hand out brochures on street corners, or to perform other time-consuming tasks that require a large number of people. Solicit their help by contacting a school principal or career counselor, or appeal to your members, who may have high school–aged children whom they can encourage to lend a hand. When you face difficulty in meeting a deadline, high school students can provide the extra energy needed to get the job done.

If yours is a nonprofit organization, you may be able to get a professional advertising agency or public relations firm to volunteer its services in support of your cause. Such firms sometimes donate their efforts to foster good relations with the community. At your request, an agency may help you plan your campaign; it may design and print posters, or it may issue PSAs or brochures. Such services are usually limited to a specific product, so don't expect the agency to take over your whole campaign for free. Once involved, however, it should be kept informed of your progress, in case its voluntary services become available in the future.

Since advertising and public relations firms are often besieged by requests for volunteer help, they are most likely to respond favorably to organizations that are established, well-known and well-organized, and working for an unquestionably worthy cause. If your organization is poorly run or has a bad reputation, an agency may advise you on how to clean up your image, but it is unlikely to offer further help until you are clearly doing as much as *you* can.

For the same reason that ad agencies volunteer their services, businesses that sell advertising space—on billboards, in subways, or in direct-mail flyers—sometimes offer it for free, and may even kick in the cost of designing and producing an ad. But, again, they donate their services only to well-known organizations promoting a social benefit. In most cities and states, various associations annually select worthy community groups, which are each awarded a billboard for one month, or even a full-page ad in a magazine. You can identify such public service programs by contacting the Ad Council of America or simply by asking someone in a local advertising agency. Remember that such free publicity should supplement, not replace, your regular activities; if the Ad Council sees that you are already very committed to your cause and effectively publicizing it, it will also be more inclined to award you free space.

Canvassing

Canvassing is simply a soliciting of votes, sales, opinions, or donations from a group or district of people. Most nonprofit groups use canvassing to solicit small donations or to raise awareness concerning a specific issue. It is the latter use we are concerned with here.

As yet another grass-roots method of reaching the public, canvassing does not rely on the print or electronic media to communicate your message; instead, it puts you one-on-one with your audience. Of all the networking techniques, it is perhaps the most difficult. This is not because it is complicated or requires special skills, but because it is personally demanding. Canvassing is physically wearing, mentally frustrating, and emotionally draining. When conducted properly, however, it can bolster your campaign, shore up uninterested neighborhoods, and boost your total membership.

There are two ways to canvass. The first is to stand on a busy street corner and approach people as they come by. You simply offer them a brochure, so that they do not have to stop but can read about your cause at their convenience. Your pitch should last only a couple of seconds—if you try to take more time than that, you are pushing your luck, especially if you are on a busy street accosting people on their way to or from work. Many canvassers fail because they try to accomplish too much. They feel they can convert a total stranger, who may hardly have been aware of their cause previously, in a matter of minutes. The worst way to canvass, especially on a street corner, is to stop people and aggressively attempt to sell them your entire program. This approach will immediately turn them off and make the job of canvassing miserable.

The canvasser's goal is simply to make people aware of (1) his organization or (2) a specific issue. I cannot overstress the phrase *make people aware*. The goal is not to convince people to join your group, or to decide to support or oppose an issue. When you address people on the street, be clear and concise:

> CANVASSER: Good afternoon, are you aware of the farm workers strike in southern California and how it will affect your food costs?
>
> CITIZEN: No [or yes].
>
> CANVASSER: If you are interested, here's a brochure telling all about it, and what you can do to help.

If the person takes the brochure, you can consider yourself successful. Those who refuse are probably not interested anyway or are better reached through a different mechanism. So why waste your time on an unreceptive audience? Occasionally you will meet people who are very interested and really want to talk, in which case you should elaborate, suggest they attend your next meeting, and put their names on your mailing list. Occasionally, too, you will meet an argumentative opponent, and you should likewise elaborate and stand up for your cause. Remain friendly, though, and avoid a heated debate. Your main objective is to reach as many people as possible.

The second way to canvass is by walking from door to door. This involves identifying certain neighborhoods, enlisting several workers, and dividing up the district. Door-to-door canvassing requires a lot more leg work, of course, than standing on a street corner. Walking up to someone's home and ringing the doorbell also requires a good deal of aplomb, because you never really know what to expect on someone else's turf. Depending on the neighborhood, canvassing can be downright dangerous—so know your territory. Use the same basic approach when ringing doorbells as when standing on the street corner. Be aware that you may be disturbing someone, and act accordingly. Be pleasant and polite, but also direct—let the person who answers know right off what you are all about and what you want. If you keep in mind that you're trying only to increase awareness of your cause, you'll probably fare much better. Your immediate goals are to avoid having the door slammed in your face, to leave your informational brochure, and to encourage the person at the door to read it.

Your spiel should again be as simple as possible:

> Good afternoon. I hope I'm not disturbing you, but I represent Citizens for Safe Energy, and we are opposing the utility rate increases that the local utilities have recently proposed to the State Commissioner. Here is a brochure that describes our program and outlines our position. If you can spare a few moments, please read it. And don't hesitate to call us if you want more information, or if you would like to get involved. Opposing these rate increases can save you money. Thank you, and good day.

Be frank; nothing will destroy your credibility faster than stumbling over words, mumbling, or acting suspicious. With the spectre of the traveling salesman accompanying anyone who attempts to solicit door-to-door, it is difficult to win trust and respect as a canvasser. You have to continually work at it.

A canvasser who came to my door recently needed a few lessons in communicating. He seemed to think trickery was the way to win support—a fatal mistake for any canvasser. Upon answering my door I was greeted by a young man who asked me to sign a petition in support of a nuclear arms freeze. Since I support the cause, I was pleased with the opportunity to sign. But as I reached for the petition he said, "Why don't you just give me your name and address and I'll write it down. I've been having trouble reading people's writing." (Strike one: he offended me by implying I might not be competent to write my name legibly. It was a minor social transgression, but a real psychological blow.) I went along with him and gave him my name and address, knowing he had lied to me. (Strike two: he said he had a petition, but I know full well that no petition is official if not personally signed. Obviously he was up to something.) Then he asked me for a donation, and when I said I might send him a check if he would give me an address to send it to, he responded, "I don't suppose you could give it to me now? Most people, when they say that, never send the check." (Strike three: this guy was burying himself by hinting that I was untrustworthy. He should have given me the information and allowed me to decide in private. I never give money to canvassers, incidentally; I always send it by mail. And as a canvasser I never accept it. To avoid giving people any reason to question your organization's credibility, always have them mail a check.) Though I was sympathetic to his cause, this canvasser struck out with me.

Canvassers never really know whom they are talking to. But there are right ways and wrong ways to address any stranger. The immediate impression you make will color your entire spiel and will often determine whether you are successful or not. Before you go through the effort of canvassing, consider what you aim to accomplish, and how you should go about accomplishing it. Put yourself in the place of the people you are soliciting: What would make *you* receptive, and what would *you* be willing to give a canvasser on the spot? Thinking this way will go a long way toward making you an effective canvasser.

Films for Loan

Films are popular with schools, clubs, and other organizations, which show them for both entertainment and edification at monthly meetings and other gatherings. Establishing a film-for-loan library can make it easy to maintain an information network with these groups. Provided your cause is not too obscure or revolutionary, you can usually locate and obtain enough relevant films—three or four, each twenty minutes long—to stock a small library. Your films needn't treat your topic specifically, but only relate to it in some way. If you were campaigning to save the Florida alligator, for example, you might obtain a film on the history of the Everglades and another on reptiles and amphibians. Your aim is to create an awareness, and the best way to do so is to coat the issues with a little entertainment. Before showing a popular and entertaining film, of course, you can say a few words about your cause to your captive audience, and afterwards you can pass out literature.

Begin by asking your public library for a list of films. You can also contact various branches of the federal government, including the Public Television Network, which often broadcasts feature films on subjects of public interest and makes them available to groups for a fee. You can often buy 16-millimeter, color films for less than one hundred dollars, athough high-quality documentaries are in the range of two to three hundred dollars. Aside from the initial cost of the films, and perhaps a projector for your own group's use, you will have to pay only for one-way postage each time a film is requested. (If you present the film yourself, of course, you can take it along with you.) Always insure films sent by mail.

If you publicize your film-for-loan library well, you will soon have many more requests than you can fill. You will also have developed a network of contacts who may open the door to future talks, members, and support. Films for loan help you maintain visibility with a minimal expense of time and money.

Mailing Lists

The people on your mailing list are your core support group —they are the informed constituency you have worked so hard to develop. You may start out with a mailing list of only forty or fifty names, but if you continue to sign people up at presentations, exhibitions, and meetings, the total may soon reach into the thousands. It is a good idea to have interested people fill out a postcard with their name, address, interests, and affiliations and send it back at their convenience. You can either alphabetize the cards or place them in zip-code order. You will then be able to add and delete entries as necessary, and categorize them according to interests, affiliations, or address when you want to contact a select group.

If you want your mailing list to grow quickly, you might piggyback your publication on another. If you were putting out your first newsletter, for instance, you might arrange with a like-minded group to include your newsletter as a supplement to its publication. You would supply the other group with copies of your newsletter, accompanied by a postcard or mailing form so interested readers could sign up to receive your newsletter in the future. You might also ask established newsletters to run a small display ad or blurb inviting people to sign up for your list. Still another tactic is to obtain existing mailing lists. You can rent them from businesses that make their living locating and trading such lists, or you can borrow them from small organizations like your own or governmental agencies. (You can get a list of state legislators, for example, from your secretary of state.) Send everyone on the existing list an introductory issue of your publication with an invitation to sign up. If you obtain other lists, either by purchase or on loan, you should be sure the people on it have related interests. You would not send a newsletter on issues pertaining to the sea to a list of people residing in Colorado.

Producing labels for your mailings can be time-consuming, particularly if you have a list of thousands. With a few hundred entries, though, you can type a master list on specially lined 8½-by-11-inch paper and photocopy it onto pre-pasted labels. By affixing copied labels to your envelopes, you can keep your master list intact for future mailings. If you have more than a few hundred entries, you'll probably want to hire a professional mailing house. It can do the job quickly and cheaply, especially if it has a computer. The mailing house works right from your postcards; each person's name and address is typed on a special data card, which is fed into a machine that prints and attaches a label to an envelope, far more quickly than any mere mortal. Having the data cards typed usually costs about twenty cents each, and this is a one-time cost. You can avoid it altogether by obtaining the data cards from the mailer and typing them yourself. Your subsequent mailings will cost about $15 to $20 per thousand.

10.

The Publicist's Library

ACCURATE information is essential to every successful publicity campaign. As a beginning publicist you should familiarize yourself with the range of standard references and guides available. You need not purchase all the books listed here, though some will be indispensable. Many are terribly expensive, and most can be found at your local library. Although this list covers most of the subjects I've discussed, it is not exhaustive. When you need extra help, don't be afraid to comb the bookshelves or badger the librarians.

General Reference

Standard's Rates and Data (5201 Old Orchard Road, Skokie, Illinois 60076) publishes a series of media directories, including *Radio Rates and Data, Television Rates and Data, Business Publication Rates and Data,* and *Consumer Magazine Rates and Data.* Collectively, these books contain a wealth of information on publicity opportunities offered by the press and electronic media. Listings are arranged by subject, as in *Consumer Magazine Rates and Data,* or by geographical area, as in *Radio Rates and Data.* Each listing includes names of key personnel, advertising rates, circulation or market, format, and frequency of publication.

U.S. Publicity Directory is a five-volume reference covering U.S. magazines, radio and television, newspapers, business and finance publications, and communications services. Each listing includes address, phone numbers, description of contents, key personnel, circulation or market, deadlines, and advertising rates. The volume on communications services lists all U.S. news bureaus, wire services, and feature syndicates, and picture research companies. The *U.S. Publicity Directory* is published twice each year, in summer and winter editions, by John Wiley and Sons, 605 Third Avenue, New York, New York 10158.

Gale Research Company (Book Tower, Detroit, Michigan 48226) publishes a number of directories of interest to the publicist. The *Encyclopedia of Associations* lists some fifteen thousand national organizations. The *Consumer Sourcebook* identifies sources of information for consumer protection and guidance, including government agencies, associations, centers, and institutes. The *Health Services Directory* lists some twenty thousand health clinics, centers, programs, and services in the United States and some foreign countries. You should also be aware of Gale's *Speakers and Lecturers: How to Find Them,* which can help you locate keynote speakers for rallies, seminars, meetings, and other events. These directories offer loads of useful information, whether you are identifying organizations with similar interests, compiling mailing lists, researching specific topics, or recruiting speakers.

Print Media

Ayer Directory of Publications is the publicist's bible. It lists nearly every newspaper (daily, weekly, biweekly, and triweekly) and every magazine (consumer, business, technical, professional, and trade) published at least four times a year in the United States or Canada, and it includes listings for Bermuda, Panama, the Philippines, and the Bahamas as well. Publications are categorized by state, city, and town. Each listing gives the publisher's address, circulation, topics covered, and coordinates that can be located on a set of special state maps. For each newspaper with a circulation of one hundred thousand or greater, features and editors are listed. A subject index enables users to identify audiences by interests. A revised edition is published annually by Ayer Press, One Bala Avenue, Bala Cynwyd, Pennsylvania 19004.

Ulrich's International Periodicals Directory is similar to the *Ayer Directory*, but it lists periodicals published throughout the world. *Ulrich's* is arranged by subject, and almost any subject you can imagine is included. Titles, addresses, contacts, publication schedules, and formats are listed for each publication. Revised biennially, *Ulrich's* is published by R. R. Bowker Company, 1180 Avenue of the Americas, New York, New York 10036. A quarterly update is issued separately.

The Directory of the College Student Press in America can help you locate newspapers and newsletters published on campuses throughout the United States. These student publications can be excellent outlets for publicity directed toward college populations; many have large circulations, and because students and professors are often easy to mobilize and take active roles in promoting social causes, the practical publicist may find important audiences among them. Revised periodically, the directory lists addresses, contacts, formats, and circulations. It is published by Oxbridge Communications, 183 Madison Avenue, New York, New York 10016.

On Reporting the News, by William Burrows, is a thorough guide to reporting and writing news stories on special topics, or "beats," such as public safety, accidents, science and technology, sports, business and finance, religion, education, courts and the law, and politics and government. It describes the theory of reporting and offers tips on information gathering. A section on the mechanics of writing includes such topics as leads, quotes, word choice, interviews, and features. This book is a must for any publicist who plans to write for or send releases to the press. It was published in 1977 by New York University Press, Washington Square, New York, New York 10003.

Reporting, by Mitchell and Blair Charnley, provides tips, examples, and thoughts on the craft of reporting. With an emphasis on local news, this is a thorough guide for young journalists or publicists who have little experience writing for the press. Appendices include guidelines on copy preparation, a code of ethics for journalists, and a glossary of journalists' jargon. *Reporting* was published in 1979 by Holt, Rinehart and Winston, 521 Fifth Avenue, sixth floor, New York, New York 10175.

The Associated Press Stylebook and Libel Manual, published in 1982 by the Associated Press Wire Service (50 Rockefeller Plaza, New York, New York 10020), is a handy reference for writing press releases. Arranged alphabetically by subject, it includes information on libel, caption writing, and "filing the wire," or transmitting stories by telegraph. For the publicist, this book offers valuable insight to how the wire services work.

Broadcast Media

Larimi Communications (151 East Fiftieth Street, New York, New York 10022) publishes several useful broadcasting directories. *TV Contacts, Radio Contacts,* and *Cable Contacts Yearbook* provide names of media contacts and descriptions of shows. These directories are revised annually, and monthly updates are available by subscription. Larimi also publishes a weekly *Contacts* newsletter, which provides the publicist with current information on both print and broadcasting outlets.

Broadcasting Yearbook, published by Broadcasting Publications (1735 DeSales Street, N.W., Washington, D.C. 20036) and revised every year, is perhaps the most comprehensive single-volume reference on the broadcasting industry. Here you can find listings, arranged by geographical market, for nearly all television and radio stations in the United States, Canada, Mexico, and the Caribbean. Each market is displayed on a map and is ranked by the size of its potential audience. Included are the stations' network affiliations, addresses, phone numbers, key personnel, and, for radio stations, types of programming. Advertising agencies, news services, personnel of the major networks, and independent producers and distributors are also listed. Information is provided on Federal Communications Commission regulations and the National Association of Broadcasters television and radio code.

Television Factbook, published by Washington Television Digest (1836 Jefferson Place, N.W., Washington, D.C. 20036), is a directory dedicated solely to television. It contains a station-by-station listing of all television outlets in the country. It identifies geographical markets, size of potential audience, ranking, address, phone numbers, and key personnel for each station. Small maps are included. Washington Television Digest also publishes *Radio Factbook*, a separate but similar reference book for radio.

Broadcast Journalism: An Introduction to News Writing, by Mark Hall, is a good, readable introduction to broadcast journalism. It covers everything from the mechanics of writing "live" copy to reporting on crime, disasters, and terrorism. It tells you how to put together a five-minute news broadcast and produce a mini-documentary, and it examines the journalist's responsibilities and the issue of good taste in broadcasting. The book was published in 1978 by

Hastings House Publishers, 10 East Fortieth Street, New York, New York 10016.

Public Speaking

The Speaker's Handy Reference, by Edward Friedman, is a straightforward guide to planning and delivering speeches and developing effective public communications skills. It includes a compendium of remarks, facts, trivia, and jokes, arranged by subject, that you may use to embellish your speeches. *The Speaker's Handy Reference* is a good source of ideas for the publicist, particularly in times of crisis. It was published in 1967 by Harper and Row, 10 East Fifty-third Street, New York, New York 10022.

Bartlett's Familiar Quotations is a hefty book of quotations from literary figures, politicians, philosophers, and other well-known persons from every age and every country. Indexed by speaker, subject, and first line, quotes from this collection can spice up your press releases, newsletter articles, citizen editorials, and speeches. *Bartlett's* was published in 1980 by Little, Brown and Company, 34 Beacon Street, Boston, Massachusetts 02106.

Government

State and Local Government, edited by Joseph Zimmerman, describes elected and appointed offices in both state and local government. Nearly every government function is covered, including interstate relations; public protection, health, and welfare; land policies and planning; political parties and pressure groups; and finance. The appendices include data on voting turnout, legislative sessions and procedures, state tax revenues, and federal aid to state and local governments. A good general guide to the maze of government, this handbook can be a great help in determining which agencies have jurisdiction over particular social matters, which officials should be notified of your group's activities, and who may be able to help your cause. It can be particularly useful in locating agencies that issue permits for demonstrations, rallies, and other public events. A must for any publicist involved with lobbying or passing legislation, *State and Local Government* is part of the Barnes and Noble Outline Series published by Harper and Row, 10 East Fifty-third Street, New York, New York 10022.

State Registers or manuals, published annually in many states, are valuable references, especially for publicity campaigns on the community level. They usually include information on state legislators (addresses, staff, committee appointments) and the executive branch (departments, agencies, key contacts). They list towns and their officials, both elected and appointed. Many contain information on the state's congressional delegation, as well as industrial history and profiles, population statistics, and descriptions of the state's economy and geography. To obtain a copy of your state's register, check with your secretary of state or state library.

Federal Staff Directory, published each year by the Congressional Directory (Mount Vernon, Virginia), lists every federal agency, commission, advisory committee, and bureau, including regional offices. Over twenty-five thousand key officials are identified, along with their offices, addresses, and phone numbers. Biographies of senior officials are provided. A subject index allows you to locate agencies and contacts by their function, interest, or area of jurisdiction. This directory is especially useful in assembling mailing lists and acquiring federal publications.

Congressional Staff Directory is a good companion to the *Federal Staff Directory*. It identifies state delegations, their staffs, and staffs of congressional committees. Biographies of senators and congressmen are included, as well as titles, addresses, and phone numbers of all congressional employees. Congressional districts and members are listed for 9,900 cities. When preparing mailing lists publicists should not overlook congressmen, particularly if they are dealing with a social or political issue, a public benefit or service, or legislation.

Graphic Design

Pocket Pal: A Graphic Arts Production Handbook is a good introduction to printing for the beginner, and a useful reference for the professional as well. It covers the history of printing, the printing process today, type and typesetting, copy preparation and art work, graphic arts photography, stripping and imposition, platemaking, binding, paper and inks, and a glossary. This little manual is a must for publicists who deal often with printers. Published by International Paper Company (220 East Forty-second Street, New York, New York 10017), *Pocket Pal* can be purchased at almost any graphic arts store.

Production for the Graphic Designer, by James Craig, is another excellent reference book for the publicist involved in printing materials. A show-and-tell guide to printing, it covers many of the same subjects as *Pocket Pal* but has a large format and many more illustrations. It is published by Watson-Guptill, a division of Billboard Publications (1515 Broadway, New York, New York 10036).

The Joy of Photography, written by the editors of the Eastman Kodak Company, is an excellent guide to the entire photographic process. Though a very readable book for the amateur, it is comprehensive and attractively illustrated. Of special interest to the publicist are sections on producing slide shows and using display photos. *The Joy of Photography* is published by Addison-Wesley, Reading, Massachusetts 01867.

Index